The Woodworker's Guide to

Shop DISCARD
Math

Tom Begnal

POPULAR WOODWORKING BOOKS
CINCINNATI, OHIO

Read This Important Safety Notice

To prevent accidents, keep safety in mind while you work. Use the safety guards installed on power equipment, keep fingers away from saw blades, wear safety goggles to prevent injuries from flying wood chips and sawdust, wear headphones to protect your hearing, and consider installing a dust vacuum to reduce the amount of airborne sawdust in your woodshop. Don't wear loose clothing, such as neckties or shirts with loose sleeves, or jewelry, such as rings, necklaces or bracelets, when working on power equipment. The author and editors who compiled this book have tried to make all the contents as accurate and correct as possible. Plans, illustrations, photographs and text have been carefully checked. All instructions, plans and projects should be carefully read, studied and understood before beginning construction. Due to the variability of local conditions, construction materials, skill levels, etc., neither the author nor Popular Woodworking Books assumes any responsibility for any accidents, injuries, damages or other losses incurred resulting from the material presented in this book.

Other fine Popular Woodworking Books are available from your local bookstore or direct from the publisher.

02   01   00   99   98   5   4   3   2   1

Library of Congress Cataloging-in-Publication Data

Begnal, Tom.
    The woodworker's guide to shop math / by Tom Begnal.
      p.   cm.
    Includes index.
    ISBN 1-55870-485-X (Pbk. : alk. paper)
    1. Woodwork—Mathematics. 2. Shop mathematics. I. Title.
TT180.B423   1998
684'.08'0151—dc21   98-18133
                                    CIP

Edited by R. Adam Blake
Content edited by Bruce E. Stoker
Production edited by Amanda Magoto
Designed by Angela Lennert Wilcox
Cover photography by Pamela Monfort Braun, Bronze Photography

Illustrations in chapter sixteen provided by the L.S. Starrett Company.

To Colleen, Kevin and Brendan

I extend my thanks to the following organizations for their valuable help with this book:

L.S. Starrett Company, Athol, Massachusetts; National Particleboard Association, Gaithersburg, Maryland; and the Western Wood Products Association, Portland, Oregon.

ABOUT THE AUTHOR

Tom Begnal is the author of *The Woodworking Handbook* (Betterway Books). He served as managing editor of *The Woodworker's Journal* magazine for over 15 years. In addition, he has written or edited woodworking and how-to books for several publishers including F&W Publications, McGraw-Hill, Rodale Press and Sterling Publishing. He lives in Kent, Connecticut.

CONTENTS

INTRODUCTION

By its very nature, woodworking is a craft that requires a basic understanding of math. After all, you use various numbers—in the form of thickness, width and length dimensions—to describe the physical size of a woodworking project and its component parts. Inevitably, many of those dimensions—written as whole numbers, fractions and decimals—must be added, subtracted, multiplied and divided in order to cut and assemble a project. And, of course, the math must be done accurately if the project is to be successfully completed.

Also, many geometric relationships can be found in the woodshop. A woodworking project and its parts consist of a variety of geometric shapes, and an understanding of that geometry can often make designing and building a project considerably easier.

A number of special math formulas can be applied to woodworking. If you know the formulas and how to use them, your time in the woodshop is going to be much more productive.

Although math is an important part of woodworking, a surprising number of woodworkers feel somewhat intimidated when working with things like fractions, decimals, geometry, formulas and other math-related exercises. However, woodshop math is not something to be feared and avoided; it simply involves understanding and applying some basic information.

The Woodworker's Guide to Shop Math provides much of that information. The book shows, in an easy-to-understand format, how to work with fractions and decimals, powers and roots, shop geometry and compound angles. It also details how to enlarge grid patterns, solve right triangles, convert photos into dimensioned drawings and apply a number of useful formulas. Much of the information is presented in a step-by-step format. In addition, a number of valuable conversion charts and an extensive table of powers and roots are included.

I hope you find that *The Woodworker's Guide to Shop Math* takes much of the mystery out of woodshop math. Once the mystery is gone, math becomes a lot easier and more enjoyable, and you'll become a better woodworker.

PART ONE

BASIC WOODSHOP ARITHMETIC

A Review of Fractions, Decimals, Powers and Roots

CHAPTER 1
Understanding Fractions

In the woodshop, you often need to work with part of a whole. For example, you might need to use part of a quart of polyurethane, not the whole quart; part of an inch, not the whole inch; part of a box of 100 screws, not the whole box of 100 screws; or part of a 4′-long pine board, not the whole board.

Before you can start doing any heavy lifting with fractions (like adding, subtracting, multiplying and dividing them), you need to understand some fraction basics. This chapter covers the fundamentals, so let's get started.

WHAT IS A FRACTION?

In short, a **fraction** is a part of a whole. As an example, let's say you cut a 4′-long board into four 1′-long pieces (Fig. 1-1). (To simplify things, we are going to forget about saw-kerf waste.) Let's also say you use two of the four 1′ lengths as drawer fronts for a hutch cupboard you are building.

Fig. 1-1

When you use two of the four 1′ lengths, you have used two parts of the whole. Written as a fraction, it looks like this:

$$\frac{2}{4}$$

Note that the fraction is made up of two parts. The bottom part is called the **denominator**, while the top part is called the **numerator**. The line between the denominator and numerator is called the **fraction line** or **fraction bar**. Sometimes the fraction line is shown as a slanted line: 2/4.

In any fraction, the denominator represents the number of equal parts that the whole has been divided into (4 in our board example), while the numerator represents the number of equal parts taken from the denominator (2 in our example).

READING FRACTIONS

When reading a fraction, you read the numerator first, followed by the denominator. Here's a list of some fractions commonly encountered in the woodshop.

$\frac{1}{2}$ = one-half, $\frac{2}{2}$ = two-halves

$\frac{1}{3}$ = one-third, $\frac{2}{3}$ = two-thirds, $\frac{3}{3}$ = three-thirds

$\frac{1}{4}$ = one-quarter, $\frac{2}{4}$ = two-quarters, $\frac{3}{4}$ = three-quarters, etc.

$\frac{1}{5}$ = one-fifth, $\frac{2}{5}$ = two-fifths, $\frac{3}{5}$ = three-fifths, etc.

$\frac{1}{6}$ = one-sixth, $\frac{2}{6}$ = two-sixths, $\frac{3}{6}$ = three-sixths, etc.

$\frac{1}{7}$ = one-seventh, $\frac{2}{7}$ = two-sevenths, $\frac{3}{7}$ = three-sevenths, etc.

$\frac{1}{8}$ = one-eighth, $\frac{2}{8}$ = two-eighths, $\frac{3}{8}$ = three-eighths, etc.

$\frac{1}{9}$ = one-ninth, $\frac{2}{9}$ = two-ninths, $\frac{3}{9}$ = three-ninths, etc.

$\frac{1}{10}$ = one-tenth, $\frac{2}{10}$ = two-tenths, $\frac{3}{10}$ = three-tenths, etc.

$\frac{1}{12}$ = one-twelfth, $\frac{2}{12}$ = two-twelfths, $\frac{3}{12}$ = three-twelfths, etc.

$\frac{1}{16}$ = one-sixteenth, $\frac{2}{16}$ = two-sixteenths, $\frac{3}{16}$ = three-sixteenths, etc.

$\frac{1}{32}$ = one-thirty-second, $\frac{2}{32}$ = two-thirty-seconds, etc.

$\frac{1}{64}$ = one-sixty-fourth, $\frac{2}{64}$ = two-sixty-fourths, etc.

FRACTIONS AND DIVISION

The symbol $\div$ and the division box ($\overline{)}\quad$) are used to indicate division. The fraction bar is also an indicator of division. Therefore, the fraction $\frac{2}{4}$ also means 2 $\div$ 4.

TYPES OF FRACTIONS

All fractions can be classified as either **proper fractions** or **improper fractions**.

PROPER FRACTIONS

Proper fractions have a numerator that is smaller than the denominator. Examples of proper fractions are: $\frac{1}{8}$, $\frac{3}{8}$, $\frac{3}{4}$, $\frac{7}{16}$, $\frac{31}{32}$ and $\frac{23}{64}$. The value of a proper fraction is always less than one. Put another way, if the denominator is divided into the numerator, the result is always less than one.

IMPROPER FRACTIONS

Improper fractions have a numerator that is equal to or greater than the denominator. Examples of improper fractions are $\frac{2}{2}$, $\frac{3}{2}$, $\frac{4}{3}$, $\frac{23}{8}$, $\frac{16}{16}$ and $\frac{67}{64}$. The value of an improper fraction is always equal to or greater than one. That means if the denominator is divided into the numerator, the result is always equal to or greater than one.

REDUCING FRACTIONS TO LOWEST TERMS

The numerator and denominator of a fraction are called the **terms** of the fraction. When working with a fraction, it is often helpful to write the fraction in its lowest terms. You'll find that a fraction in its lowest terms is usually easier to use.

A fraction written in its lowest terms is called a **reduced fraction** and is said to be in its **simplest form**. The procedure for reducing a fraction to its lowest terms is sometimes called **simplifying** a fraction.

Let's look again at our example using the 4'-long board (Fig. 1-2). As you can see from the illustration, $\frac{2}{4}$ of the board is also equal to $\frac{1}{2}$. Changing $\frac{2}{4}$ to $\frac{1}{2}$ reduces the fraction to its lowest terms, although the value of the fraction remains the same.

Fig. 1-2

Let's look at another example and consider a 12'-long board that's cut into 1' lengths (Fig. 1-3). If you use four of the twelve 1' lengths, you have used four parts of the whole. Written as a fraction, it looks like this:

$$\frac{4}{12}$$

But as the illustration shows, the fraction $\frac{4}{12}$ is also equal to $\frac{1}{3}$. Changing $\frac{4}{12}$ to $\frac{1}{3}$ reduces the fraction to its lowest terms, yet the value remains the same: $\frac{4}{12}$ of the board is the same as $\frac{1}{3}$ of the board.

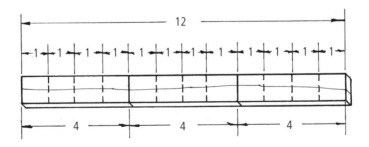

Fig. 1-3

While an illustration is handy for helping us see how a fraction can be reduced to lowest terms, it's not the most practical method for doing the work. Let's use some examples to show you another way.

Example 1: Reduce the fraction $\frac{6}{8}$ to lowest terms.

STEP 1: Look at the fraction and determine the *largest* number that divides evenly into *both* the numerator and the denominator. Usually, this step takes some guessing and a bit of trial and error.

For this example, my thinking goes something like this: Both terms are even numbers, so I know 2 is a possibility. But is there a number *larger* than 2 that will divide evenly into *both* terms? The numbers 3 and 6 divide into the numerator (6) but not into the denominator (8). The number 4 divides into the denominator (8), but not the numerator (6). The numbers 5 and 7 won't divide evenly into either term, so 2 is the number.

STEP 2: Divide the numerator and denominator by 2.

$$\frac{6 \div 2}{8 \div 2} = \frac{3}{4}$$

The fraction $\frac{6}{8}$ reduced to lowest terms is $\frac{3}{4}$.

Example 2: Reduce the fraction $\frac{21}{30}$ to lowest terms.

STEP 1: Look at the fraction and determine the largest number that divides evenly into both the numerator and the denominator. The numerator is not an even number, so neither 2 nor any even number is a possibility. The number 3 divides evenly into both the numerator (21) and the denominator (30), so it is a possibility. The numbers 5, 9, 11, 13, 15, 17 and 19 won't divide into the numerator (21), and the number 7 won't divide into the denominator, so 3 is the number.

STEP 2: Divide the numerator and denominator by 3.

$$\frac{21 \div 3}{30 \div 3} = \frac{7}{10}$$

The fraction $\frac{21}{30}$ reduced to lowest terms is $\frac{7}{10}$.

Example 3: Reduce the fraction $\frac{9}{16}$ to lowest terms.

STEP 1: Look at the fraction and determine the largest number that divides evenly into both the numerator and the denominator. The numerator is not an even number, so even numbers are not candidates. The number 3 divides evenly into the numerator (9) but not the denominator (16). The numbers 5 and 7 won't divide into either term. The number 9 divides into the numerator (9) but not the denominator (16). Therefore, the fraction $\frac{9}{16}$ cannot be reduced to lower terms.

RAISING FRACTIONS TO HIGHER TERMS

When working with fractions, it is sometimes necessary to raise a fraction to higher terms. The procedure is pretty straightforward: You simply multiply both the numerator and denominator by a **common number**, sometimes called a **common multiplier**. Let's use the fraction $\frac{5}{8}$ and a common number of 4.

$$\frac{5 \times 4}{8 \times 4} = \frac{20}{32}$$

Indeed, you can multiply the numerator and denominator by any common number and the fraction will be raised to higher terms.

$$\frac{5 \times 2}{8 \times 2} = \frac{10}{16} \text{ and } \frac{5 \times 6}{8 \times 6} = \frac{30}{48} \text{ and } \frac{5 \times 21}{8 \times 21} = \frac{105}{168}$$

EQUIVALENT FRACTIONS

We now know that when a fraction is reduced to its lowest terms (for example, $\frac{4}{6}$ to $\frac{2}{3}$), the original and reduced fractions have the same value. We also know that when a fraction is raised to higher terms (for example, $\frac{1}{4}$ to $\frac{3}{12}$), the original and raised fractions also have the same value. Fractions that have the same value are called **equivalent fractions**. The fractions $\frac{1}{2}, \frac{2}{4}, \frac{4}{8}, \frac{8}{16}, \frac{16}{32}$ and $\frac{32}{64}$ are examples of equivalent fractions because they all have the same value.

MAKING A WHOLE NUMBER A FRACTION

You can turn any whole number into a fraction. To do it, simply write the whole number as the numerator and write the number 1 as the denominator. For example, to make the number 7 a fraction, write 7 as the numerator and 1 as the denominator. The fraction looks like this:

$$\frac{7}{1}$$

Here are a few more examples:

Whole Number	Whole Number as a Fraction
1	$\frac{1}{1}$
5	$\frac{5}{1}$
14	$\frac{14}{1}$
137	$\frac{137}{1}$

COMMON DENOMINATORS

When doing certain operations—like adding and subtracting—with two or more fractions, all the fractions must have the same denominator. Fractions with the same denominator are said to have a **common denominator**. More specifically, a common denominator is a number that is evenly divisible by the denominators of all the fractions you are using. Let's look at an example.

Example 1: Find a common denominator for the fractions $\frac{1}{3}$ and $\frac{4}{9}$, then write equivalent fractions using the common denominator.

STEP 1: If possible, reduce one or both of the fractions to lowest terms. In this case, neither fraction can be reduced.

STEP 2: To produce a common denominator, multiply the denominator of one fraction times the denominator of the second: $3 \times 9 = 27$. Therefore, a common denominator for these fractions is 27.

STEP 3: Raise both fractions to higher terms using the common denominator. To raise $\frac{1}{3}$ to higher terms with a denominator of 27, use 9 as the common number.

$$\frac{1 \times 9}{3 \times 9} = \frac{9}{27}$$

To raise $\frac{4}{9}$ to higher terms with a denominator of 27, use 3 as the common number.

$$\frac{4 \times 3}{9 \times 3} = \frac{12}{27}$$

The number 27 is a common denominator for the fractions $\frac{1}{3}$ and $\frac{4}{9}$. The equivalent fractions are $\frac{9}{27}$ (for $\frac{1}{3}$) and $\frac{12}{27}$ (for $\frac{4}{9}$).

LOWEST COMMON DENOMINATOR

It's not unusual for two or more fractions to have more than one common denominator. In the example we just looked at, in addition to the number 27, the numbers 9, 18, 36, 45 and 54 are some of the other possible common denominators.

When working with fractions, it is sometimes easier to use the **lowest common denominator**, also called the **LCD**. The lowest common denominator is the *smallest* number that is evenly divisible by the denominators of all the fractions you are using. In the example we just did, the number 9 is the lowest common denominator. To find out how to find the LCD, let's look at a couple examples.

Example 1: Find the lowest common denominator for the fractions $\frac{1}{8}$ and $\frac{5}{6}$, then write the equivalent fractions using that denominator.

STEP 1: If possible, reduce one or both of the fractions to lowest terms. In this case, neither fraction can be reduced.

STEP 2: Next, check to see if the largest denominator (8 in our example) can serve as the lowest common denominator for the fractions. It can't, so you must do some more looking.

The process of finding the LCD takes a bit of trial and error. You know that you can find a common denominator simply by multiplying the two denominators ($8 \times 6 = 48$). But in this case, you want the lowest common denominator, which might or might not be 48.

To find the LCD, begin by multiplying the largest denominator (8) by 2: $8 \times 2 = 16$. Check to see if both denominators divide evenly into 16. Since 8 does and 6 doesn't, multiply the largest denominator by 3: $8 \times 3 = 24$. Do both denominators divide evenly into 24? Bingo, they do, so the lowest common denominator is 24.

STEP 3: Raise the fractions to higher terms with the lowest common denominator. To raise $\frac{1}{8}$ to a higher term that has a denominator of 24, use 3 as the common number.

$$\frac{1 \times 3}{8 \times 3} = \frac{3}{24}$$

To raise $\frac{5}{6}$ to a higher term that has a denominator of 24, use 4 as the common number.

$$\frac{5 \times 4}{6 \times 4} = \frac{20}{24}$$

The number 24 is the lowest common denominator for the fractions $\frac{1}{8}$ and $\frac{5}{6}$. The equivalent fractions are $\frac{3}{24}$ and $\frac{20}{24}$.

Example 2: Find the lowest common denominator for the fractions $\frac{2}{6}$, $\frac{3}{8}$ and $\frac{7}{12}$, then write the equivalent fractions using that denominator.

STEP 1: If possible, reduce the fractions to lowest terms. In this case, the fraction $\frac{2}{6}$ can be reduced.

$$\frac{2 \div 2}{6 \div 2} = \frac{1}{3}$$

The new fraction group is now $\frac{1}{3}$, $\frac{3}{8}$ and $\frac{7}{12}$.

STEP 2: Check to see if the largest denominator (12 in this example) can serve as the lowest common denominator for all three fractions. It can't, so you must keep looking.

You can find a common denominator simply by multiplying the three denominators ($3 \times 8 \times 12 = 288$), but you are looking for the lowest common denominator, which might or might not be 288.

To find the LCD, begin by multiplying the largest denominator (12) by 2: $12 \times 2 = 24$. See if the other two denominators divide evenly into 24. They do, so the lowest common denominator is 24.

STEP 3: Raise the fractions to higher terms with the lowest common denominator. To raise $\frac{1}{3}$ to a higher term that has a denominator of 24, use 8 as the common number.

$$\frac{1 \times 8}{3 \times 8} = \frac{8}{24}$$

To raise $\frac{3}{8}$ to higher terms with a denominator of 24, use 3 as the common number.

$$\frac{3 \times 3}{8 \times 3} = \frac{9}{24}$$

To raise $\frac{7}{12}$ to higher terms with a denominator of 24, use 2 as the common number.

$$\frac{7 \times 2}{12 \times 2} = \frac{14}{24}$$

The number 24 is the lowest common denominator for the fractions $\frac{2}{6}$, $\frac{3}{8}$ and $\frac{7}{12}$. The equivalent fractions are $\frac{8}{24}$, $\frac{9}{24}$ and $\frac{14}{24}$.

LIKE FRACTIONS AND UNLIKE FRACTIONS

Fractions with a common denominator are called **like fractions**. The fractions $\frac{1}{16}$, $\frac{3}{16}$, $\frac{8}{16}$, $\frac{12}{16}$ and $\frac{15}{16}$ are examples of like fractions because they all have the number 16 as a denominator.

Fractions with different denominators are called **unlike fractions**. The fractions $\frac{3}{4}$, $\frac{3}{8}$, $\frac{9}{16}$ and $\frac{12}{32}$ are examples of unlike fractions.

COMPARING LIKE FRACTIONS

When fractions have a common denominator, it's easy to determine which one is biggest. For example, let's say you have a pair of 1-gallon containers partially filled with wood stain; one is $\frac{5}{8}$ full and the other is $\frac{7}{8}$ full. Which one has more stain? When you have like fractions the answer is easy: The fraction with the largest numerator always represents the largest fraction—in this case, $\frac{7}{8}$.

COMPARING UNLIKE FRACTIONS

Let's say we find a couple more 1-gallon containers partially filled with stain. One is $\frac{3}{4}$ full; the other is $\frac{9}{16}$ full. Which one has more stain?

In this case, the fractions are unlike, so you can't simply compare the numerators to find out which container has the most stain. Instead, you must convert one or both fractions so they have a common denominator, then you can compare the numerators.

First, if possible, reduce the fractions to lowest terms. This step usually makes the next steps easier. In this case, however, both fractions are already at their lowest terms.

Next, check to see if the larger denominator (16 in our example) can serve as a common denominator for both fractions. If it can, it's going to save some work. In this case, the denominator of 4 can be divided into 16, which means the fraction $\frac{3}{4}$ can be raised to higher terms with 16 as the denominator.

Now, raise the fraction $\frac{3}{4}$ to higher terms so the equivalent fraction has a denominator of 16. Using a common number of 4 produces a denominator of 16.

$$\frac{3 \times 4}{4 \times 4} = \frac{12}{16}$$

With the denominators the same, you are able to compare the fractions in question: $\frac{12}{16}$ and $\frac{9}{16}$. As discussed earlier, when you have like fractions, the fraction with the largest numerator always represents the largest fraction—in this case, $\frac{12}{16}$. Therefore, the container that's $\frac{3}{4}$ full has more stain.

Let's look at one more example and use a step-by-step procedure to determine which is bigger: $\frac{1}{4}$ or $\frac{4}{6}$.

STEP 1: If possible, reduce the fractions to lowest terms. Looking at the two fractions here, you can see that the fraction $\frac{1}{4}$ can't be reduced. However, $\frac{4}{6}$ can be reduced by dividing both the numerator and denominator by 2.

$$\frac{4 \div 2}{6 \div 2} = \frac{2}{3}$$

Now let's compare the fractions $\frac{1}{4}$ and $\frac{2}{3}$.

STEP 2: Next, check to see if the larger denominator (4 in our example) can serve as a common denominator for the fractions. Since it can't, you must find a common denominator, so multiply the denominator of one fraction by the denominator of the second: $4 \times 3 = 12$. Therefore, a common denominator for both fractions is 12.

STEP 3: Raise the fractions to higher terms with 12 as a denominator. To raise $\frac{1}{4}$ to higher terms with a denominator of 12, use 3 as the common number.

$$\frac{1 \times 3}{4 \times 3} = \frac{3}{12}$$

To raise $\frac{2}{3}$ to higher terms with a denominator of 12, use 4 as the common number.

$$\frac{2 \times 4}{3 \times 4} = \frac{8}{12}$$

STEP 4: Compare the like fractions $\frac{3}{12}$ and $\frac{8}{12}$.
The fraction $\frac{8}{12}$ is greater than $\frac{3}{12}$. Therefore, $\frac{4}{6}$ is greater than $\frac{1}{4}$.

MIXED NUMBERS

Sometimes a whole number is combined with a fraction. A number that contains both a whole number and a proper fraction is called a **mixed number**. Examples of mixed numbers are $1\frac{1}{4}$, $5\frac{7}{8}$, $12\frac{1}{2}$ and $47\frac{17}{32}$.

Mixed numbers are directly related to improper fractions. Indeed, mixed numbers can be converted easily to improper fractions, and improper fractions can be changed easily to mixed numbers.

CHANGING IMPROPER FRACTIONS TO MIXED NUMBERS

You will recall that the fraction line is an indicator of division. When doing division, the number to be divided is called the **dividend**, while the number by which we divide is called the **divisor**. The number that results is called the **quotient**.

Changing an improper fraction to a mixed number is pretty simple: You need only divide the numerator by the denominator. Let's look at a couple examples:

Example 1: Change the improper fraction $\frac{9}{2}$ to a mixed number.

STEP 1: Divide 9 by 2.

$$\begin{array}{r} 4 \\ 2\overline{)9} \\ \underline{8} \\ 1 \end{array} \text{ (remainder)}$$

STEP 2: Write the quotient as a whole number (4), then write the remainder (1) and divisor (2) as a fraction, with the remainder as the numerator and the divisor as the denominator. If necessary, reduce the fraction to its lowest terms.

$$\begin{array}{r} 4 \\ 2\overline{)9} \\ \underline{8} \\ 1 \end{array} = 4\frac{1}{2} \quad \text{ (remainder)}$$

The fraction $\frac{1}{2}$ is already at its lowest terms. Therefore, the improper fraction $\frac{9}{2}$ equals the mixed number $4\frac{1}{2}$.

Example 2: Change the improper fraction $\frac{26}{8}$ to a mixed number.

STEP 1: Divide 26 by 8.

$$
\begin{array}{r}
3 \\
8)\overline{26} \\
\underline{24} \\
2 \quad \text{(remainder)}
\end{array}
$$

STEP 2: Write the quotient as a whole number (3), then write the remainder (2) and divisor (8) as a fraction, with the remainder as the numerator and the divisor as the denominator. If necessary, reduce the fraction to its lowest terms.

$$
\begin{array}{r}
3 \\
8)\overline{26} \\
\underline{24} \\
2 \quad \text{(remainder)}
\end{array}
\quad = 3\frac{2}{8}
$$

Reduce the fraction $\frac{2}{8}$ to its lowest terms:

$$
\frac{2 \div 2}{8 \div 2} = \frac{1}{4}
$$

The improper fraction $\frac{26}{8}$ equals the mixed number $3\frac{1}{4}$.

CHANGING MIXED NUMBERS TO IMPROPER FRACTIONS

When working with fractions, you'll sometimes need to change a mixed number to an improper fraction. Here are a few examples that show how to do it.

Example 1: Convert $4\frac{2}{3}$ to an improper fraction.

Create a new numerator by multiplying the denominator of the fraction (3) by the whole number (4) then adding the numerator of the fraction (2). The denominator remains the same.

$$
4\frac{2}{3} = \frac{(3 \times 4) + 2}{3} = \frac{12 + 2}{3} = \frac{14}{3}
$$

The mixed number $4\frac{2}{3}$ is equal to the fraction $\frac{14}{3}$.

Example 2: Convert $11\frac{5}{8}$ to an improper fraction.

As in Example 1, create a new numerator by multiplying the denominator the fraction by the whole number then adding the numerator of the action. Keep the same denominator.

$$
11\frac{5}{8} = \frac{(8 \times 11) + 5}{8} = \frac{88 + 5}{8} = \frac{93}{8}
$$

The mixed number $11\frac{5}{8}$ is equal to the fraction $\frac{93}{8}$.

CHAPTER 2

Working With Fractions

Fractions seem to be as much a part of woodworking as a well-cut dovetail joint. Parts of things are constantly being added, subtracted, multiplied and divided. We add fractions of an inch, subtract fractions of a meter, multiply fractions of a pound and divide fractions of an angle. No doubt, a good understanding of how to work with fractions can make your time in the woodshop more productive.

If fractions have intimidated you in the past, take heart. This chapter will show you how to solve just about any problem that involves a fraction.

ADDING FRACTIONS

The addition of fractions is the most common operation involving fractions. The examples that follow show how to add like fractions, unlike fractions and mixed numbers.

ADDING LIKE FRACTIONS

As you know, two or more fractions with a common denominator are called like fractions. The procedure for adding like fractions is pretty basic: You simply add all the numerators and write the sum over the common denominator. Then, if possible, reduce the new fraction to its lowest terms. Let's look at some examples.

Example 1: Add $\frac{1}{8}$ and $\frac{3}{8}$.

STEP 1: Write the problem.

$$\frac{1}{8} + \frac{3}{8} =$$

STEP 2: Add all the numerators and write the numerator sum: $1 + 3 = 4$.

$$\frac{1}{8} + \frac{3}{8} = \frac{4}{} \text{ (numerator sum)}$$

STEP 3: Write the common denominator (8) under the numerator sum.

$$\frac{1}{8} + \frac{3}{8} = \frac{4}{8} \text{ (common denominator)}$$

STEP 4: If possible, reduce the sum to lowest terms.

$$\frac{4 \div 4}{8 \div 4} = \frac{1}{2}$$

Therefore, $\frac{1}{8} + \frac{3}{8} = \frac{1}{2}$.

Example 2: Add $\frac{7}{12}$ and $\frac{5}{12}$.

STEP 1: Write the problem.

$$\frac{7}{12} + \frac{5}{12} =$$

STEP 2: Add all the numerators and write the numerator sum: $7 + 5 = 12$.

$$\frac{7}{12} + \frac{5}{12} = \frac{12}{}$$

STEP 3: Write the common denominator (12) under the numerator sum.

$$\frac{7}{12} + \frac{5}{12} = \frac{12}{12}$$

STEP 4: If possible, reduce the sum to lowest terms. From chapter one, you know that any number divided by itself is equal to 1.

$$\frac{12}{12} = 1$$

Therefore, $\frac{7}{12} + \frac{5}{12} = 1$.

Example 3: Add $\frac{5}{16}$, $\frac{7}{16}$ and $\frac{9}{16}$.

STEP 1: Write the problem.

$$\frac{5}{16} + \frac{7}{16} + \frac{9}{16} =$$

STEP 2: Add all the numerators and write the numerator sum: $5 + 7 + 9 = 21$.

$$\frac{5}{16} + \frac{7}{16} + \frac{9}{16} = \frac{21}{}$$

STEP 3: Write the common denominator (16) under the numerator sum.

$$\frac{5}{16} + \frac{7}{16} + \frac{9}{16} = \frac{21}{16}$$

STEP 4: Since the sum $\frac{21}{16}$ is an improper fraction, change the improper fraction to a mixed number (as described in chapter one).

$$\begin{array}{r} 1 \\ 16\overline{)21} \\ \underline{16} \\ 5 \end{array} \text{ (remainder)}$$

Therefore, $\frac{5}{16} + \frac{7}{16} + \frac{9}{16} = \frac{21}{16} = 1\frac{5}{16}$.

ADDING MIXED NUMBERS THAT HAVE LIKE FRACTIONS

Mixed numbers that have like fractions are added in much the same way as like fractions. You add the whole numbers first, then add the like fractions. Let's look at a few examples.

Example 1: Add $2\frac{3}{8}$ and $5\frac{1}{8}$.

STEP 1: Write the problem.

$$2\frac{3}{8} + 5\frac{1}{8} =$$

STEP 2: Add the whole numbers: $2 + 5 = 7$.

$$2\frac{3}{8} + 5\frac{1}{8} = 7$$

STEP 3: Add the numerators of the fractions: $3 + 1 = 4$.

$$2\frac{3}{8} + 5\frac{1}{8} = 7^4$$

STEP 4: Write the common denominator (8) under the numerator.

$$2\frac{3}{8} + 5\frac{1}{8} = 7\frac{4}{8}$$

STEP 5: If possible, reduce the fraction to lowest terms.

$$\frac{4 \div 4}{8 \div 4} = \frac{1}{2}$$

Therefore, $2\frac{3}{8} + 5\frac{1}{8} = 7\frac{4}{8} = 7\frac{1}{2}$.

Example 2: Add $3\frac{7}{16}$ and $5\frac{9}{16}$.

STEP 1: Write the problem.

$$3\frac{7}{16} + 5\frac{9}{16} =$$

STEP 2: Add the whole numbers: $3 + 5 = 8$.

$$3\frac{7}{16} + 5\frac{9}{16} = 8$$

STEP 3: Add the fraction numerators: $7 + 9 = 16$.

$$3\frac{7}{16} + 5\frac{9}{16} = 8^{16}$$

STEP 4: Write the common denominator (16) under the numerator.

$$3\frac{7}{16} + 5\frac{9}{16} = 8\frac{16}{16}$$

STEP 5: If possible, reduce the fraction to lowest terms. From chapter one, you know that any number divided by itself is equal to 1.

$$\frac{16}{16} = 1$$

STEP 6: The reduced fraction produces a whole number of 1, so add the whole numbers: $8 + 1 = 9$.

$$3\tfrac{7}{16} + 5\tfrac{9}{16} = 8\tfrac{16}{16} = 8 + 1 = 9$$

Therefore, $3\tfrac{7}{16} + 5\tfrac{9}{16} = 9$.

Example 3: Add $6\tfrac{1}{8}$, $2\tfrac{5}{8}$ and $4\tfrac{7}{8}$.

STEP 1: Write the problem.

$$6\tfrac{1}{8} + 2\tfrac{5}{8} + 4\tfrac{7}{8} =$$

STEP 2: Add the whole numbers: $6 + 2 + 4 = 12$.

$$6\tfrac{1}{8} + 2\tfrac{5}{8} + 4\tfrac{7}{8} = 12$$

STEP 3: Add the fraction numerators: $1 + 5 + 7 = 13$.

$$6\tfrac{1}{8} + 2\tfrac{5}{8} + 4\tfrac{7}{8} = 12\tfrac{13}{\quad}$$

STEP 4: Write the common denominator (8) under the numerator.

$$6\tfrac{1}{8} + 2\tfrac{5}{8} + 4\tfrac{7}{8} = 12\tfrac{13}{8}$$

STEP 5: Since the sum $\tfrac{13}{8}$ is an improper fraction, change the improper fraction to a mixed number.

$$\begin{array}{r} 1 \\ 8\overline{)13} \\ \underline{8} \\ 5 \quad \text{(remainder)} \end{array}$$

The improper fraction $\tfrac{13}{8}$ is equal to the mixed number $1\tfrac{5}{8}$.

STEP 6: Add the whole number (12) and mixed number ($1\tfrac{5}{8}$).

$$12 + 1\tfrac{5}{8} = 13\tfrac{5}{8}$$

Therefore, $6\tfrac{1}{8} + 2\tfrac{5}{8} + 4\tfrac{7}{8} = 13\tfrac{5}{8}$.

ADDING UNLIKE FRACTIONS

From chapter one, you know that unlike fractions are fractions that have different denominators. Unlike fractions can be added, but first they must be changed to fractions that have common denominators. (If necessary, review chapter one to see how to find a common denominator for unlike fractions.)

Let's look at an example.

Example: Add $\frac{1}{2}$ and $\frac{3}{8}$.

STEP 1: Write the problem.

$$\frac{1}{2} + \frac{3}{8} =$$

STEP 2: Determine the lowest common denominator.
   The lowest common denominator is 8.

STEP 3: Raise the fraction $\frac{1}{2}$ to higher terms with the common denominator 8, using 4 as the common number.

$$\frac{1 \times 4}{2 \times 4} = \frac{4}{8}$$

STEP 4: Add the like fractions.

$$\frac{4}{8} + \frac{3}{8} = \frac{7}{8}$$

Therefore, $\frac{1}{2} + \frac{3}{8} = \frac{7}{8}$.

ADDING MIXED NUMBERS THAT HAVE UNLIKE FRACTIONS

Mixed numbers that have unlike fractions are added in much the same way as unlike fractions. You convert the unlike fractions to like fractions before adding the whole numbers and the fractions. Let's look at an example.

Example: Add $5\frac{3}{16}$ and $3\frac{1}{4}$.

STEP 1: Write the problem.

$$5\frac{3}{16} + 3\frac{1}{4} =$$

STEP 2: Determine the lowest common denominator.
   The lowest common denominator is 16.

STEP 3: Raise the fraction $\frac{1}{4}$ to higher terms with the common denominator 16, using 4 as the common number.

$$\frac{1 \times 4}{4 \times 4} = \frac{4}{16}$$

STEP 4: Rewrite the problem.

$$5\frac{3}{16} + 3\frac{4}{16} =$$

STEP 5: Add the whole numbers.

$$5\frac{3}{16} + 3\frac{4}{16} = 8$$

STEP 6: Add the fractions.

$$5\tfrac{3}{16} + 3\tfrac{4}{16} = 8\tfrac{7}{16}$$

Therefore, $5\tfrac{3}{16} + 3\tfrac{1}{4} = 8\tfrac{7}{16}$.

SUBTRACTING FRACTIONS

The subtraction of fractions is probably the second most common operation involving fractions. The examples that follow show how to subtract like fractions, unlike fractions and mixed numbers.

SUBTRACTING LIKE FRACTIONS

Subtracting like fractions is a pretty easy procedure. You simply subtract the numerators and write the sum over the common denominator. Then, if possible, reduce the new fraction to its lowest terms. Let's look at a couple examples.

Example 1: Subtract $\tfrac{3}{8}$ from $\tfrac{5}{8}$.

STEP 1: Write the problem.

$$\frac{5}{8} - \frac{3}{8} =$$

STEP 2: Subtract the numerators: $5 - 3 = 2$.

$$\frac{5}{8} - \frac{3}{8} = \frac{2}{}$$

STEP 3: Write the common denominator (8) under the difference.

$$\frac{5}{8} - \frac{3}{8} = \frac{2}{8}$$

STEP 4: If possible, reduce the sum to lowest terms.

$$\frac{2 \div 2}{8 \div 2} = \frac{1}{4}$$

Therefore, $\tfrac{5}{8} - \tfrac{3}{8} = \tfrac{1}{4}$.

Example 2: Subtract $\tfrac{11}{32}$ from $\tfrac{45}{32}$.

STEP 1: Write the problem.

$$\frac{45}{32} - \frac{11}{32} =$$

STEP 2: Subtract the numerators: $45 - 11 = 34$.

$$\frac{45}{32} - \frac{11}{32} = \frac{34}{}$$

STEP 3: Write the common denominator (32) under the difference.

$$\frac{45}{32} - \frac{11}{32} = \frac{34}{32}$$

STEP 4: If possible, reduce to lowest terms.

$$\frac{34 \div 2}{32 \div 2} = \frac{17}{16}$$

STEP 5: Change the improper fraction $\frac{17}{16}$ to a mixed number (if necessary, see chapter one for review).

$$\frac{17}{16} = 1\frac{1}{16}$$

Therefore, $\frac{45}{32} - \frac{11}{32} = 1\frac{1}{16}$.

EXCHANGING TO SUBTRACT MIXED NUMBERS WITH LIKE FRACTIONS

Let's look at an example to see how to do this kind of subtraction.

Example: Subtract $4\frac{5}{8}$ from $8\frac{3}{8}$.

STEP 1: Write the problem.

$$8\frac{3}{8} - 4\frac{5}{8} =$$

STEP 2: Subtract the numerators.

Since 5 is greater than 3, exchange the whole number 8 for the whole number 7 plus the fraction $\frac{8}{8}$ (we know that $7 + \frac{8}{8} = 8$). The problem now looks like this:

$$8\frac{3}{8} - 4\frac{5}{8} = \left(7\frac{8}{8} + \frac{3}{8}\right) - 4\frac{5}{8} = 7\frac{11}{8} - 4\frac{5}{8}$$

Now the numerators can be subtracted: $11 - 5 = 6$.

$$7\frac{11}{8} - 4\frac{5}{8} = \frac{6}{}$$

STEP 3: Write the common denominator (8) under the numerator difference.

$$7\frac{11}{8} - 4\frac{5}{8} = \frac{6}{8}$$

STEP 4: Subtract the whole numbers: $7 - 4 = 3$.

$$7\frac{11}{8} - 4\frac{5}{8} = 3\frac{6}{8}$$

STEP 5: If possible, reduce the fraction to lowest terms.

$$\frac{6 \div 2}{8 \div 2} = \frac{3}{4}$$

Therefore, $8\frac{3}{8} - 4\frac{5}{8} = 3\frac{3}{4}$.

SUBTRACTING UNLIKE FRACTIONS

Unlike fractions can be subtracted, but first they must be changed to fractions that have common denominators. (If necessary, review chapter one to see how to find a common denominator for unlike fractions.)

Example: Subtract $\frac{5}{16}$ from $\frac{7}{8}$.

STEP 1: Write the problem.

$$\frac{7}{8} - \frac{5}{16} =$$

STEP 2: Determine the lowest common denominator.
    The lowest common denominator is 16.

STEP 3: Raise the fraction $\frac{7}{8}$ to higher terms with the common denominator 16, using 2 as the common number.

$$\frac{7 \times 2}{8 \times 2} = \frac{14}{16}$$

STEP 4: Subtract the like fractions.

$$\frac{14}{16} - \frac{5}{16} = \frac{9}{16}$$

Therefore, $\frac{7}{8} - \frac{5}{16} = \frac{9}{16}$.

EXCHANGING TO SUBTRACT MIXED NUMBERS WITH UNLIKE FRACTIONS

Example: Subtract $15\frac{11}{16}$ from $28\frac{5}{32}$.

STEP 1: Write the problem.

$$28\frac{5}{32} - 15\frac{11}{16}$$

STEP 2: Determine the lowest common denominator.
    The lowest common denominator is 32.

STEP 3: Raise the fraction $\frac{11}{16}$ to higher terms with the common denominator 32, using 2 as the common number.

$$\frac{11 \times 2}{16 \times 2} = \frac{22}{32}$$

STEP 4: Rewrite the problem with the common denominator.

$$28\frac{5}{32} - 15\frac{22}{32} =$$

STEP 5: Subtract the numerators.

Since 22 is greater than 5, exchange the whole number 28 for the whole number 27 plus the fraction $\frac{32}{32}$ (we know that $27 + \frac{32}{32} = 28$). The problem now looks like this:

$$28\tfrac{5}{32} - 15\tfrac{22}{32} = \left(27\tfrac{32}{32} + \tfrac{5}{32}\right) - 15\tfrac{22}{32} = 27\tfrac{37}{32} - 15\tfrac{22}{32}$$

Now the numerators can be subtracted: $37 - 22 = 15$.

$$27\tfrac{37}{32} - 15\tfrac{22}{32} = \tfrac{15}{}$$

STEP 6: Write the common denominator (32) under the numerator difference.

$$27\tfrac{37}{32} - 15\tfrac{22}{32} = \tfrac{15}{32}$$

STEP 7: Subtract the whole numbers: $27 - 15 = 12$.

$$27\tfrac{37}{32} - 15\tfrac{22}{32} = 12\tfrac{15}{32}$$

Therefore, $28\tfrac{5}{32} - 15\tfrac{11}{16} = 12\tfrac{15}{32}$.

MULTIPLYING FRACTIONS

In the woodshop, there are plenty of opportunities to multiply fractions. The examples that follow show how to multiply a fraction by a fraction, a fraction by a whole number and a fraction by a mixed number.

MULTIPLYING A FRACTION BY A FRACTION

To do this type of multiplication, you simply calculate numerator times numerator and denominator times denominator. Let's look at an example.

Example: Multiply $\frac{1}{2}$ by $\frac{13}{16}$.

STEP 1: Write the problem:

$$\frac{1}{2} \times \frac{13}{16}$$

STEP 2: Multiply the numerators.

$$\frac{1}{2} \times \frac{13}{16} = \frac{13}{}$$

STEP 3: Multiply the denominators.

$$\frac{1}{2} \times \frac{13}{16} = \frac{13}{32}$$

STEP 4: If possible, reduce the fraction to lowest terms.

The fraction $\frac{13}{32}$ can't be reduced.

Therefore, $\frac{1}{2} \times \frac{13}{16} = \frac{13}{32}$.

CANCELING

Fraction multiplication can often be simplified by using a procedure called **canceling**. When it can be used, canceling effectively reduces the fractions to lower terms right from the start. This makes for easier multiplication and often eliminates the need to reduce the fraction at the end of the procedure. Let's look at an example.

Example: Multiply $\frac{2}{5}$ by $\frac{3}{4}$.

STEP 1: Write the problem.

$$\frac{2}{5} \times \frac{3}{4}$$

STEP 2: Cancel, if possible, by finding a common number that can divide evenly into any numerator and any denominator.

In this problem, the common number 2 divides into the numerator 2 and the denominator 4.

$$\frac{\overset{1}{\cancel{2}}}{5} \times \frac{3}{\underset{2}{\cancel{4}}}$$

STEP 3: Multiply the numerators.

$$\frac{\overset{1}{\cancel{2}}}{5} \times \frac{3}{\underset{2}{\cancel{4}}} = \frac{3}{\_}$$

STEP 4: Multiply the denominators.

$$\frac{\overset{1}{\cancel{2}}}{5} \times \frac{3}{\underset{2}{\cancel{4}}} = \frac{3}{10}$$

The product $\frac{3}{10}$ can't be reduced; therefore, $\frac{2}{5} \times \frac{3}{4} = \frac{3}{10}$.

MULTIPLYING A FRACTION BY A WHOLE NUMBER

Recall from chapter one that a whole number can be changed into a fraction by writing the whole number as the numerator and using 1 as the denominator.

Example: Multiply $\frac{1}{4}$ by 9.

STEP 1: Write the problem.

$$\frac{1}{4} \times \frac{9}{1}$$

STEP 2: Cancel, if possible.

No common number besides 1 can divide evenly into both numerator and denominator; therefore, no cancelation can be done.

STEP 3: Multiply the numerators.

$$\frac{1}{4} \times \frac{9}{1} = \frac{9}{}$$

STEP 4: Multiply the denominators.

$$\frac{1}{4} \times \frac{9}{1} = \frac{9}{4}$$

STEP 5: If possible, reduce the fraction to lowest terms.

The fraction $\frac{9}{4}$ can't be reduced.

STEP 6: Change the improper fraction into a mixed number.

$$\begin{array}{r} 2 \\ 4\overline{)9} \\ \underline{8} \\ 1 \end{array}$$

Therefore, $\frac{1}{4} \times 9 = 2\frac{1}{4}$.

MULTIPLYING MORE THAN TWO FRACTIONS

Any number of fractions can be multiplied. The procedure is basically the same as that used to multiply a pair of fractions.

Example: Multiply $\frac{3}{4}$ by $\frac{2}{5}$ by $\frac{1}{6}$.

STEP 1: Write the problem.

$$\frac{3}{4} \times \frac{2}{5} \times \frac{1}{6}$$

STEP 2: Cancel, if possible.

The common number 2 divides into the numerator 2 and the denominator 4. Also, the common number 3 divides into the numerator 3 and the denominator 6.

$$\frac{\overset{1}{\cancel{3}}}{\underset{2}{\cancel{4}}} \times \frac{\overset{1}{\cancel{2}}}{5} \times \frac{1}{\underset{2}{\cancel{6}}}$$

STEP 3: Multiply the numerators.

$$\frac{\overset{1}{\cancel{3}}}{\underset{2}{\cancel{4}}} \times \frac{\overset{1}{\cancel{2}}}{5} \times \frac{1}{\underset{2}{\cancel{6}}} = \frac{1}{}$$

STEP 4: Multiply the denominators.

$$\frac{\cancel{3}^{1}}{\cancel{4}_{2}} \times \frac{\cancel{2}^{1}}{5} \times \frac{1}{\cancel{6}_{2}} = \frac{1}{20}$$

Therefore, $\frac{3}{4} \times \frac{2}{5} \times \frac{1}{6} = \frac{1}{20}$.

MULTIPLYING MIXED NUMBERS

To multiply mixed numbers, first change the mixed numbers to improper fractions. After multiplying, change the improper fractions back to mixed numbers. If necessary, review chapter one to see how to change mixed numbers to improper fractions and vice versa.

Example: Multiply $3\frac{1}{6}$ by $2\frac{2}{5}$.

STEP 1: Write the problem.

$$3\frac{1}{6} \times 2\frac{2}{5}$$

STEP 2: Change the mixed numbers to improper fractions.

$$3\frac{1}{6} = \frac{19}{6} \qquad 2\frac{2}{5} = \frac{12}{5}$$

STEP 3: Rewrite the problem.

$$\frac{19}{6} \times \frac{12}{5}$$

STEP 4: Cancel, if possible.
   The common number 6 divides into the numerator 12 and the denominator 6.

$$\frac{19}{\cancel{6}_{1}} \times \frac{\cancel{12}^{2}}{5}$$

STEP 5: Multiply the numerators.

$$\frac{19}{\cancel{6}_{1}} \times \frac{\cancel{12}^{2}}{5} = \frac{38}{}$$

STEP 6: Multiply the denominators.

$$\frac{19}{\cancel{6}_{1}} \times \frac{\cancel{12}^{2}}{5} = \frac{38}{5}$$

STEP 7: Change the improper fraction to a mixed number.

$$\begin{array}{r} 7 \\ 5\overline{)38} \\ \underline{35} \\ 3 \end{array}$$

Therefore, $3\frac{1}{6} \times 2\frac{2}{5} = 7\frac{3}{5}$.

DIVIDING FRACTIONS

The examples that follow show how to divide a fraction by a fraction, a whole number by a fraction, and how to divide mixed numbers.

DIVIDING A FRACTION BY A FRACTION

The procedure for dividing one fraction by another is pretty straightforward. You simply invert the **divisor** (the number by which we divide) and then multiply the fractions. Let's look at an example.

Example: Divide $\frac{3}{4}$ by $\frac{7}{8}$.

STEP 1: Write the problem.

$$\frac{3}{4} \div \frac{7}{8}$$

The fraction $\frac{7}{8}$ is the divisor, since it is the number by which we divide.

STEP 2: Invert the divisor and change the operation from division to multiplication.

$$\frac{3}{4} \times \frac{8}{7}$$

STEP 3: Cancel, if possible.
  The common number 4 divides into the numerator 8 and the denominator 4.

$$\frac{3}{\cancel{4}_1} \times \frac{\cancel{8}^2}{7}$$

STEP 4: Multiply the numerators.

$$\frac{3}{\cancel{4}_1} \times \frac{\cancel{8}^2}{7} = \frac{6}{\_}$$

STEP 5: Multiply the denominators.

$$\frac{3}{\cancel{4}_1} \times \frac{\cancel{8}^2}{7} = \frac{6}{7}$$

Therefore, $\frac{3}{4} \div \frac{7}{8} = \frac{6}{7}$.

DIVIDING A WHOLE NUMBER BY A FRACTION

To divide a whole number by a fraction, first write the whole number as a fraction, then invert the divisor and multiply the fractions. Here's how it works.

Example: Divide 9 by $\frac{3}{4}$.

STEP 1: Write the problem, showing the whole number as a fraction.

$$\frac{9}{1} \div \frac{3}{4}$$

STEP 2: Invert the divisor and change the operation from division to multiplication.

$$\frac{9}{1} \times \frac{4}{3}$$

STEP 3: Cancel, if possible.

The common number 3 divides into the numerator 9 and the denominator 3.

$$\frac{\overset{3}{\cancel{9}}}{1} \times \frac{4}{\underset{1}{\cancel{3}}}$$

STEP 4: Multiply the numerators.

$$\frac{\overset{3}{\cancel{9}}}{1} \times \frac{4}{\underset{1}{\cancel{3}}} = \frac{12}{}$$

STEP 5: Multiply the denominators.

$$\frac{\overset{3}{\cancel{9}}}{1} \times \frac{4}{\underset{1}{\cancel{3}}} = \frac{12}{1}$$

Therefore, $9 \div \frac{3}{4} = 12$.

DIVIDING MIXED NUMBERS

To divide mixed numbers, change the mixed numbers to improper fractions, then invert the divisor and multiply the fractions.

Example: Divide $3\frac{5}{8}$ by $2\frac{1}{4}$.

STEP 1: Write the problem.

$$3\frac{5}{8} \div 2\frac{1}{4}$$

STEP 2: Change the mixed numbers to improper fractions.

$$3\frac{5}{8} = \frac{29}{8} \qquad 2\frac{1}{4} = \frac{9}{4}$$

STEP 3: Rewrite the problem.

$$\frac{29}{8} \div \frac{9}{4}$$

STEP 4: Invert the divisor and change the operation from division to multiplication.

$$\frac{29}{8} \times \frac{4}{9}$$

STEP 5: Cancel, if possible.
The common number 4 divides into the numerator 4 and the denominator 8.

$$\frac{29}{\cancel{8}} \times \frac{\cancel{4}^{1}}{9}$$
$$_{2}$$

STEP 6: Multiply the numerators.

$$\frac{29}{\cancel{8}_{2}} \times \frac{\cancel{4}^{1}}{9} = \frac{29}{}$$

STEP 7: Multiply the denominators.

$$\frac{29}{\cancel{8}_{2}} \times \frac{\cancel{4}^{1}}{9} = \frac{29}{18}$$

STEP 8: Change the improper fraction to a mixed number.

$$\begin{array}{r} 1 \\ 18\overline{)29} \\ \underline{18} \\ 11 \end{array}$$

Therefore, $3\frac{5}{8} \div 2\frac{1}{4} = 1\frac{11}{18}$.

WOODSHOP APPLICATION
Working With Fractions

You are building an Early American wall shelf that must measure $32\frac{7}{8}''$ in height (Fig. 2-1) to fit the available space. The four shelves, which each measure $\frac{13}{16}''$ thick, are to be spaced $10\frac{5}{8}''$, $8\frac{3}{8}''$ and $6\frac{1}{2}''$ apart to accommodate your collection of hardcover and softcover books. From a visual standpoint, it's important for the space at the top and bottom of the wall shelf (dimension A) to be the same. What is dimension A?

Fig. 2-1

To find A, determine the distance between the bottom of the bottom shelf and the top of the top shelf (dimension B), then subtract B from $32\frac{7}{8}''$ and divide the result by 2.

STEP 1: Find the total thickness for all four shelves.
There are four shelves, each one $\frac{13}{16}''$ thick, so multiply 4 by $\frac{13}{16}$ to find the total thickness for all four shelves.
First, change the whole number 4 to a fraction $(\frac{4}{1})$ and write the problem.

$$\frac{4}{1} \times \frac{13}{16} = \frac{52}{16}$$

Cancel.

$$\frac{\overset{1}{\cancel{4}}}{1} \times \frac{13}{\underset{4}{\cancel{16}}} = \frac{13}{4}$$

Change the improper fraction to a mixed number.

$$\begin{array}{r} 3 \\ 4\overline{)13} \\ \underline{12} \\ 1 \end{array} \qquad = 3\frac{1}{4}$$

Therefore, $4 \times \frac{13}{16}'' = 3\frac{1}{4}''$.

STEP 2: Find dimension B by adding the total thickness for all four shelves ($3\frac{1}{4}$) plus the distance between each of the shelves.

$$3\frac{1}{4} + 10\frac{5}{8} + 8\frac{3}{8} + 6\frac{1}{2} =$$

Since this addition problem involves mixed numbers with unlike fractions, you'll need to find the lowest common denominator.

The lowest common denominator is 8.

Raise the fraction $\frac{1}{4}$ to higher terms with the common denominator 8, using 2 as the common number.

$$\frac{1 \times 2}{4 \times 2} = \frac{2}{8}$$

Raise the fraction $\frac{1}{2}$ to higher terms with the common denominator 8, using 4 as the common number.

$$\frac{1 \times 4}{2 \times 4} = \frac{4}{8}$$

Rewrite the problem and add.

$$3\frac{2}{8} + 10\frac{5}{8} + 8\frac{3}{8} + 6\frac{4}{8} = 28\frac{6}{8} = 28\frac{3}{4}$$

Dimension B $= 28\frac{3}{4}''$.

STEP 3: Subtract B from $32\frac{7}{8}$ inches.

$$32\frac{7}{8} - 28\frac{3}{4} =$$

Since this subtraction problem involves mixed numbers with unlike fractions, you'll need to find the lowest common denominator.

The lowest common denominator is 8.

Raise the fraction $\frac{3}{4}$ to higher terms with the common denominator 8, using 2 as the common number.

$$\frac{3 \times 2}{4 \times 2} = \frac{6}{8}$$

Rewrite the problem and subtract.

$$32\frac{7}{8} - 28\frac{6}{8} = 4\frac{1}{8}$$

Therefore, $32\frac{7}{8}'' - 28\frac{3}{4}'' = 4\frac{1}{8}''$.

STEP 4: Divide $4\frac{1}{8}$ by 2.

$$4\frac{1}{8} \div 2$$

Convert the mixed number into an improper fraction and rewrite the problem.

$$4\frac{1}{8} = \frac{33}{8}$$

$$\frac{33}{8} \div 2$$

Write the problem with the whole number as a fraction.

$$\frac{33}{8} \div \frac{2}{1}$$

Invert the divisor and multiply.

$$\frac{33}{8} \times \frac{1}{2} = \frac{33}{16}$$

Change the improper fraction into a mixed number.

$$16\overline{)33} \quad = 2\frac{1}{16}$$
$$\underline{32}$$
$$1$$

Therefore, $A = 2\frac{1}{16}''$.

CHAPTER 3

Understanding Decimals

You know from chapter one that a fraction represents a part of a whole. But in our system of numbers, a fraction isn't the only way to show part of a whole. A **decimal** can also be used to show that a whole is made up of smaller parts. A decimal is simply a means of expressing a fraction that has a denominator of 10 or some multiple of 10. Fractions can be converted to decimals, and decimals can be converted to fractions.

Any positive number that can be expressed without a fraction or a decimal is called a **whole number**. A **mixed decimal** is a number consisting of a whole number and a decimal. A period mark (.), called the **decimal point**, is used to separate the whole number from the decimal. Any number to the left of a decimal point is a whole number, while any number to the right of a decimal point is a decimal. For example, in the number 6.5, the number 6 is a whole number and the number .5 is a decimal. To look at it another way, any number to the left of the decimal point has a value of one or more, and any number to the right of the decimal point has a value of less than one.

A whole number is understood to have a decimal point at the end of the number, although the decimal point is not usually shown. We simply write 23, not 23., for example.

PLACE VALUE AND DECIMALS

Our system of arithmetic is based on the number ten. We create all our numbers by collecting smaller numbers into groups of ten or multiples of ten. For example, the number 26 can be considered as two groups of ten plus a group of six ones.

$$26 = 2 \text{ tens } + 6 \text{ ones}$$

or

$$26 = 20 + 6$$

The number 598 can be considered as five groups of 100 (a multiple of ten) plus nine groups of ten plus a group of 8 ones.

$$598 = 5 \text{ hundreds } + 9 \text{ tens } + 8 \text{ ones}$$

or

$$598 = 500 + 90 + 8$$

A number broken down into its component groups of ten or multiples of ten is said to be in **expanded form**.

The value of a digit depends upon its location, or place, in a number. The location of a digit in a number is called its **place value**. In the number 37, the digit 7 has a different place value than it does in the number 79. In the number 37, the digit 7 represents seven ones, or 7; in the number 79, the digit 7 represents 7 tens, or 70.

THE PLACE VALUE CHART

Place value can best be shown using a chart. In the chart, each column heading represents a place value. Move one column to the left and the place value is increased ten times. Move one column to the right and you have one-tenth the previous place value. For example, move one column to the left of the thousands place value and the value becomes ten thousand. But, move one column the right of the thousands place value and you have a value of one hundred.

As mentioned earlier, the values to the right of the decimal point are less than one. The first column to the right of the decimal point represents tenths ($\frac{1}{10}$ or .1). Any number in that column has a value in tenths. Therefore, when considering the decimal .3, you know that its value is equal to three-tenths, or $\frac{3}{10}$, since the number 3 is in the tenths column. A decimal that extends to the tenths column is called a **one-place decimal**.

The column immediately to the right of the tenths column represents hundredths ($\frac{1}{100}$ or .01). Any number extending to that column has a value in hundredths. So, when considering the decimal .31, you know its value is equal to thirty-one hundredths, or $\frac{31}{100}$, since the number 31 extends to the hundredths column. A decimal that extends to the hundredths column is called a **two-place decimal**.

The column immediately to the right of the hundredths columns represents thousandths ($\frac{1}{1000}$ or .001). Any number in that column has a value in thousandths. When you see the decimal .547, you see that the number 547 extends to the thousandths column, so its value equals five-hundred forty-seven thousandths, or $\frac{547}{1000}$. A decimal that extends to the thousandths column is called a **three-place decimal**.

Page space limits the number of place values shown, but no limit to the number of place values that can be used exists. Columns can be continually added to the left side of the decimal point to provide place values for numbers greater than one, like ten million, one hundred million, one billion, and so on. Also, columns can be added to the right side of the decimal point to provide place values for numbers less than one, like ten-millionths, hundred-millionths, billionths, etc. In woodworking, however, it's rare to work beyond the hundredths place when using decimals.

Place Value Chart

Millions	Hundred Thousands	Ten Thousands	Thousands	Hundreds	Tens	Ones	Decimal Point	Tenths	Hundredths	Thousandths	Ten Thousandths	Hundred Thousandths	Millionths
							.						

Let's use the place value chart to consider the whole number 30,624.

Place Value Chart

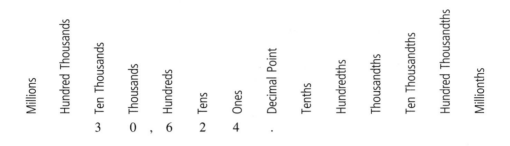

Millions	Hundred Thousands	Ten Thousands	Thousands	Hundreds	Tens	Ones	Decimal Point	Tenths	Hundredths	Thousandths	Ten Thousandths	Hundred Thousandths	Millionths
		3	0 ,	6	2	4	.						

Written in expanded form, the number 30,624 looks like this:

30,624 = 3 ten thousands + 0 thousands + 6 hundreds + 2 tens + 4 ones

or

3 ten thousands	=	3 ×	10,000	=	30,000
0 thousands	=	0 ×	1,000	=	0,000
6 hundreds	=	6 ×	100	=	600
2 tens	=	2 ×	10	=	20
4 ones	=	4 ×	1	=	4
TOTAL				=	30,624

Now, let's use the place value chart to look at the decimal number .476328.

Place Value Chart

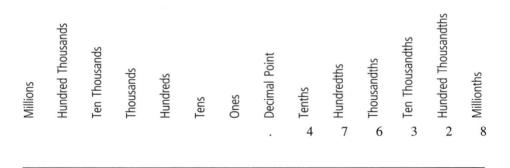

Millions	Hundred Thousands	Ten Thousands	Thousands	Hundreds	Tens	Ones	Decimal Point	Tenths	Hundredths	Thousandths	Ten Thousandths	Hundred Thousandths	Millionths
							.	4	7	6	3	2	8

Written in expanded form, the number .476328 looks like this:

.476328 = 4 tenths + 7 hundredths + 6 thousandths + 3 ten thousandths

+ 2 hundred thousandths + 8 millionths

or

4 tenths	$= 4 \times \frac{1}{10}$	$= 4 \times .1$	$= .4$
7 hundredths	$= 7 \times \frac{1}{100}$	$= 7 \times .01$	$= .07$
6 thousandths	$= 6 \times \frac{1}{1000}$	$= 6 \times .001$	$= .006$
3 ten thousandths	$= 3 \times \frac{1}{10,000}$	$= 3 \times .0001$	$= .0003$
2 hundred thousandths	$= 2 \times \frac{1}{100,000}$	$= 2 \times .00001$	$= .00002$
8 millionths	$= 8 \times \frac{1}{1,000,000}$	$= 8 \times .000001$	$= .000008$
TOTAL			$= .476328$

By the way, the decimal .476328 is read as four hundred seventy-six thousand, three hundred twenty-eight millionths or as point four seven six three two eight.

Let's look at a few other examples of decimal place values.

.2	=	$\frac{2}{10}$
.7	=	$\frac{7}{10}$
.06	=	$\frac{6}{100}$
.37	=	$\frac{37}{100}$
.89	=	$\frac{89}{100}$
.009	=	$\frac{9}{1000}$
.020	=	$\frac{29}{1000}$
.104	=	$\frac{104}{1000}$

ZERO AS A PLACEHOLDER

A zero (or zeros) located immediately to the right of the decimal point in a decimal number serves an important purpose. The zero keeps the number in its proper place. For example, to indicate three-thousandths, two zeros are placed between the decimal point and the number 3, resulting in the decimal .003. Without the two zeros, the decimal would be written .3, which we know is three-tenths, not three-thousandths.

ADDING ZERO TO THE END OF A DECIMAL

Adding a zero to the right of a decimal number does not change its value. Therefore, 6.5 = 6.50 = 6.500 = 6.5000 = 6.50000, and so on.

COMPARING DECIMALS

As you will recall from chapter one, it isn't always easy to quickly compare fractions. Let's say, for example, you want to know if $\frac{9}{16}$ is greater than $\frac{29}{64}$. To make the comparison, you need to find the common denominator. In this case it's 64. Then, you must change $\frac{9}{16}$ to an equivalent fraction with 64 as the denominator, or $\frac{36}{64}$. Now, with both fractions having a common denominator, you can compare the fractions and see that $\frac{36}{64}$ ($\frac{9}{16}$) is greater than $\frac{29}{64}$.

Unlike fractions, it's relatively painless to compare the size of decimals because it's easy to find the common denominator. Let's look at a few examples.

Example 1: Is .3 greater than or less than .27?

$$.3 = .30 = \frac{30}{100}$$

$$.27 = \frac{27}{100}$$

Since $\frac{30}{100}$ is greater than $\frac{27}{100}$, .3 is greater than .27.

Example 2: Is .64 greater than or less than .083?

$$.64 = .640 = \frac{640}{1000}$$

$$.083 = \frac{83}{1000}$$

Since, $\frac{640}{1000}$ is greater than $\frac{83}{1000}$, .64 is greater than .083.

Example 3: Is .009 greater than or less than .0156?

$$.009 = .0090 = \frac{90}{10,000}$$

$$.0156 = \frac{156}{10,000}$$

Since $\frac{90}{10,000}$ is less than $\frac{156}{10,000}$, .009 is less than .0156.

CHANGING A DECIMAL TO A FRACTION

To change a decimal into a fraction:

STEP 1: Produce the numerator by writing the decimal number without the decimal point and without any placeholders.

STEP 2: Produce the denominator by writing the appropriate number (which will be 10 or some multiple of 10) based on the place value of the decimal.

STEP 3: If possible, reduce the fraction to lowest terms. Let's look at a few examples.

Example 1: Change .8 to a fraction.

STEP 1: Remove the decimal point and write the decimal number.

$$8$$

STEP 2: Since the decimal of .8 is in the tenths place value, the denominator is 10.

$$\frac{8}{10}$$

STEP 3: In this case, the fraction can be reduced.

$$\frac{8 \div 2}{10 \div 2} = \frac{4}{5}$$

Therefore, the decimal .8 equals the fraction $\frac{8}{10}$, or $\frac{4}{5}$.

Example 2: Change .27 to a fraction.

STEP 1: Remove the decimal point and write the decimal number.

$$\underline{27}$$

STEP 2: Since the decimal of .27 is in the hundredths place value, the denominator is 100.

$$\frac{27}{100}$$

STEP 3: In this case, the fraction can't be reduced.
    Therefore, the decimal .27 equals the fraction $\frac{27}{100}$.

Example 3: Change .375 to a fraction.

STEP 1: Remove the decimal point and write the decimal number.

$$\underline{375}$$

STEP 2: Since the decimal of .375 is in the thousandths place value, the denominator is 1000.

$$\frac{375}{1000}$$

STEP 3: In this case, the fraction can be reduced.

$$\frac{375 \div 125}{1000 \div 125} = \frac{3}{8}$$

Therefore, the decimal .375 equals the fraction $\frac{375}{1000}$, or $\frac{3}{8}$.

CHANGING A FRACTION TO A DECIMAL

To change a fraction to a decimal, divide the numerator by the denominator. Chapter four explains this type of division.

CHAPTER 4
Working With Decimals

Decimals, like fractions, can be added, subtracted, multiplied and divided. This chapter shows how to perform these operations.

ADDING DECIMALS

The procedure for adding decimals is straightforward: First, you write the numbers in column form with the decimal points aligned vertically, then you add the numbers in the same way that whole numbers are added. A decimal point is placed in the total so it aligns vertically with the decimal points in the numbers you are adding. Here are a couple examples.

Example 1: Add .25 and .31.

STEP 1: Write the numbers in column form with the decimal points aligned vertically.

$$
\begin{array}{r}
.25 \\
+ \ .31 \\
\end{array}
$$

STEP 2: Add the numbers.

$$
\begin{array}{r}
.25 \\
+ \ .31 \\
\hline
56 \\
\end{array}
$$

STEP 3: Place the decimal point in the total so it aligns vertically with the other decimal points.

$$
\begin{array}{r}
.25 \\
+ \ .31 \\
\hline
.56 \\
\end{array}
$$

Example 2: Add .324, .251 and .124.

STEP 1: Write the numbers in column form with the decimal point aligned vertically.

$$
\begin{array}{r}
.324 \\
.251 \\
+ \ .124 \\
\end{array}
$$

STEP 2: Add the numbers.

$$
\begin{array}{r}
.324 \\
.251 \\
+ \ .124 \\
\hline
699 \\
\end{array}
$$

STEP 3: Place the decimal point in the total so it aligns vertically with the other decimal points.

$$\begin{array}{r} .324 \\ .251 \\ + \ .124 \\ \hline .699 \end{array}$$

ADDING MIXED DECIMALS

You will recall from chapter three that a mixed decimal is a number consisting of a whole number and a decimal. Let's look at a couple examples to see how to add them.

Example 1: Add 12.38 and 5.76.

STEP 1: Write the numbers in column form with the decimal point aligned vertically.

$$\begin{array}{r} 12.38 \\ + \ 5.76 \\ \hline \end{array}$$

STEP 2: Add the numbers.

$$\begin{array}{r} 12.38 \\ + \ 5.76 \\ \hline 18 \ 14 \end{array}$$

STEP 3: Place the decimal point in the total so it aligns vertically with the other decimal points.

$$\begin{array}{r} 12.38 \\ + \ 5.76 \\ \hline 18.14 \end{array}$$

Example 2: Add 7.29 and .48.

STEP 1: Write the numbers in column form with the decimal points aligned vertically.

$$\begin{array}{r} 7.29 \\ + \ .48 \\ \hline \end{array}$$

STEP 2: Add the numbers.

$$\begin{array}{r} 7.29 \\ + \ .48 \\ \hline 7 \ 77 \end{array}$$

STEP 3: Place the decimal point in the total so it aligns vertically with the other decimal points.

$$\begin{array}{r} 7.29 \\ + \ .48 \\ \hline 7.77 \end{array}$$

ADDING WHEN THE DECIMAL HAS ZEROS

From chapter three, you will recall that a zero to the left of a decimal number serves as an important placeholder for the number.

Example 1: Add .05 and .22.

STEP 1: Write the numbers in column form with the decimals points aligned vertically.

$$
\begin{array}{r}
.05 \\
+\ .22 \\
\end{array}
$$

STEP 2: Add the numbers.

$$
\begin{array}{r}
.05 \\
+\ .22 \\
\hline
27 \\
\end{array}
$$

STEP 3: Place the decimal point in the total so it aligns vertically with the other decimal points.

$$
\begin{array}{r}
.05 \\
+\ .22 \\
\hline
.27 \\
\end{array}
$$

Example 2: Add .007 and .305.

STEP 1: Write the numbers in column form with the decimal points aligned vertically.

$$
\begin{array}{r}
.007 \\
+\ .305 \\
\end{array}
$$

STEP 2: Add the numbers.

$$
\begin{array}{r}
.007 \\
+\ .305 \\
\hline
312 \\
\end{array}
$$

STEP 3: Place the decimal point in the total so it aligns vertically with the other decimal points.

$$
\begin{array}{r}
.007 \\
+\ .305 \\
\hline
.312 \\
\end{array}
$$

Also from chapter three, remember that adding a zero to the right of a decimal number does not change its value.

Example 1: Add .75 and .384.

STEP 1: Write the numbers in column form with the decimal points aligned vertically.

$$
\begin{array}{r}
.75 \\
+\ .384 \\
\end{array}
$$

STEP 2: Since .384 is a three-place decimal, convert .75 into a three-place decimal by adding a zero. (This step is optional since a zero is understood to exist.)

$$
\begin{array}{r}
.750 \\
+\ .384 \\
\end{array}
$$

STEP 3: Add the numbers.

$$
\begin{array}{r}
.750 \\
+\ .384 \\
\hline
1\ 134 \\
\end{array}
$$

STEP 4: Place the decimal point in the total so it aligns vertically with the other decimal points.

$$
\begin{array}{r}
.750 \\
+\ .384 \\
\hline
1.134 \\
\end{array}
$$

Note that in this example the addition of two decimal fractions results in a mixed decimal.

Example 1: Add .005, .5026 and .3.

STEP 1: Write the numbers in column form with the decimal points aligned vertically.

$$
\begin{array}{r}
.005 \\
.5026 \\
+\ .3 \\
\hline
\end{array}
$$

STEP 2: Since .5026 is a four-place decimal, change .005 and .3 into four-place decimals by adding zeros as needed.

$$
\begin{array}{r}
.0050 \\
.5026 \\
+\ .3000 \\
\end{array}
$$

STEP 3: Add the numbers.

$$
\begin{array}{r}
.0050 \\
.5026 \\
+\ .3000 \\
\hline
8076 \\
\end{array}
$$

STEP 4: Place the decimal point in the total so it aligns vertically with the other decimal points.

$$
\begin{array}{r}
.0050 \\
.5026 \\
+\ .3000 \\
\hline
.8076 \\
\end{array}
$$

SUBTRACTING DECIMALS

Decimal numbers are subtracted much like whole numbers are subtracted. First you write the numbers in column form, keeping the decimal points aligned vertically, then you subtract the numbers to produce a difference. The decimal point is placed in the difference so it aligns vertically with decimal points in the numbers you are subtracting.

Example 1: Subtract .43 from .76.

STEP 1: Write the numbers in column form with the decimal points aligned vertically.

$$
\begin{array}{r}
.76 \\
- \ .43 \\
\end{array}
$$

STEP 2: Subtract the numbers.

$$
\begin{array}{r}
.76 \\
- \ .43 \\
\hline
33 \\
\end{array}
$$

STEP 3: Place the decimal point in the difference so it aligns vertically with the other decimal points.

$$
\begin{array}{r}
.76 \\
- \ .43 \\
\hline
.33 \\
\end{array}
$$

Example 2: Subtract .648 from .765.

STEP 1: Write the numbers in column form with the decimal points aligned vertically.

$$
\begin{array}{r}
.765 \\
- \ .648 \\
\end{array}
$$

STEP 2: Subtract the numbers.

$$
\begin{array}{r}
.765 \\
- \ .648 \\
\hline
117 \\
\end{array}
$$

STEP 3: Place the decimal point in the difference so it aligns vertically with the other decimal points.

$$
\begin{array}{r}
.765 \\
- \ .648 \\
\hline
.117 \\
\end{array}
$$

SUBTRACTING MIXED DECIMALS

A mixed decimal is subtracted in the same manner as a decimal number is subtracted.

Example 1: Subtract 128.697 from 483.953.

STEP 1: Write the numbers in column form with the decimal points aligned vertically.

$$
\begin{array}{r}
483.953 \\
- \ 128.697 \\
\end{array}
$$

STEP 2: Subtract the numbers.

$$
\begin{array}{r}
483.953 \\
- \ 128.697 \\
\hline
355 \ 256 \\
\end{array}
$$

STEP 3: Place the decimal point in the difference so it aligns vertically with the other decimal points.

$$
\begin{array}{r}
483.953 \\
- \ 128.697 \\
\hline
355.256 \\
\end{array}
$$

Example 2: Subtract .28 from 7.15.

STEP 1: Write the numbers in column form with the decimal points aligned vertically.

$$
\begin{array}{r}
7.15 \\
- \ .28 \\
\end{array}
$$

STEP 2: Subtract the numbers.

$$
\begin{array}{r}
7.15 \\
- \ .28 \\
\hline
6 \ 87 \\
\end{array}
$$

STEP 3: Place the decimal point in the difference so it aligns vertically with the other decimal points.

$$
\begin{array}{r}
7.15 \\
- \ .28 \\
\hline
6.87 \\
\end{array}
$$

SUBTRACTING WHEN THE DECIMAL HAS ZEROS AS PLACEHOLDERS

A zero between the decimal point and a decimal number serves to keep the number in its proper place value.

Example 1: Subtract .08 from .59.

STEP 1: Write the numbers in column form with the decimal points aligned vertically.

$$
\begin{array}{r}
.59 \\
- \ .08 \\
\end{array}
$$

STEP 2: Subtract the numbers.

$$\begin{array}{r} .59 \\ - \ .08 \\ \hline 51 \end{array}$$

STEP 3: Place the decimal point in the difference so it aligns vertically with the other decimal points.

$$\begin{array}{r} .59 \\ - \ .08 \\ \hline .51 \end{array}$$

Example 2: Subtract .005 from .602.

STEP 1: Write the numbers in column form with the decimal points aligned vertically.

$$\begin{array}{r} .602 \\ - \ .005 \\ \hline \end{array}$$

STEP 2: Subtract the numbers.

$$\begin{array}{r} .602 \\ - \ .005 \\ \hline 597 \end{array}$$

STEP 3: Place the decimal point in the difference so it aligns vertically with the other decimal points.

$$\begin{array}{r} .602 \\ - \ .005 \\ \hline .597 \end{array}$$

Example 3: Subtract .4 from .756.

STEP 1: Write the numbers in column form with the decimal points aligned vertically.

$$\begin{array}{r} .756 \\ - \ .4 \ \ \\ \hline \end{array}$$

STEP 2: Since .756 is a three-place decimal, make .4 a three-place decimal by adding two zeros. (This step is optional, since the zeros are understood to exist.)

$$\begin{array}{r} .756 \\ - \ .400 \\ \hline \end{array}$$

STEP 3: Subtract the numbers.

$$\begin{array}{r} .756 \\ - \ .400 \\ \hline 356 \end{array}$$

STEP 4: Place the decimal point in the difference so it aligns vertically with the other decimal points.

$$\begin{array}{r} .756 \\ -\ .400 \\ \hline .356 \end{array}$$

Example 4: Subtract .69243 from .95.

STEP 1: Write the numbers in column form with the decimal points aligned vertically.

$$\begin{array}{r} .95 \\ -\ .69243 \end{array}$$

STEP 2: Since .69243 is a five-place decimal, change .95 into a five-place decimal by adding three zeros.

$$\begin{array}{r} .95000 \\ -\ .69243 \end{array}$$

STEP 3: Subtract the numbers.

$$\begin{array}{r} .95000 \\ -\ .69243 \\ \hline 25757 \end{array}$$

STEP 4: Place the decimal point in the difference so it aligns vertically with the other decimal points.

$$\begin{array}{r} .95000 \\ -\ .69243 \\ \hline .25757 \end{array}$$

MULTIPLYING DECIMALS

Decimal numbers are multiplied in the same manner as whole numbers. Unlike adding or subtracting decimals, there is no need to vertically align the decimal points of the numbers being multiplied. Keep in mind that the number of decimal places in the product must equal the total number of decimal places in the numbers being multiplied. Here are some examples.

Example 1: Multiply .34 by .7.

STEP 1: Write the numbers.

$$\begin{array}{r} .34 \\ \times\ .7 \end{array}$$

STEP 2: Multiply the numbers as you would whole numbers.

$$\begin{array}{r} .34 \\ \times\ .7 \\ \hline 238 \end{array}$$

STEP 3: Place the decimal point in the product.

Since .34 is a two-place decimal and .7 is a one-place decimal, the total number of decimal places in the numbers being multiplied is three. Therefore, the number of decimal places in the product must equal three. Counting three decimal places from right to left, the product becomes .238.

$$
\begin{array}{r}
.34 \\
\times\ .7 \\
\hline
.238
\end{array}
$$

Example 2: Multiply .632 by .85.

STEP 1: Write the numbers.

$$
\begin{array}{r}
.632 \\
\times\ .85 \\
\hline
\end{array}
$$

STEP 2: Multiply the numbers as you would whole numbers.

$$
\begin{array}{r}
.632 \\
\times\ .85 \\
\hline
3160 \\
5056 \\
\hline
53720
\end{array}
$$

STEP 3: Place the decimal point in the product.

Since .632 is a three-place decimal and .85 is a two-place decimal, the total number of decimal places in the numbers being multiplied is five. Therefore, the number of decimal places in the product must equal five. Counting five decimal places from right to left, the product becomes .53720.

$$
\begin{array}{r}
.632 \\
\times\ .85 \\
\hline
3160 \\
5056 \\
\hline
.53720
\end{array}
$$

Example 3: Multiply .08 by .5.

STEP 1: Write the numbers.

$$
\begin{array}{r}
.08 \\
\times\ .5 \\
\hline
\end{array}
$$

STEP 2: Multiply the numbers as you would whole numbers.

$$
\begin{array}{r}
.08 \\
\times\ .5 \\
\hline
40
\end{array}
$$

STEP 3: Place the decimal point in the product.

Since .08 is a two-place decimal and .5 is a one-place decimal, the total number of decimal places in the numbers being multiplied is three. Therefore, the number of decimal places in the product must equal three. Counting three decimal places from right to left, the product becomes .040. Note that a zero must be inserted to create the three-place decimal.

$$\begin{array}{r} .08 \\ \times\ .5 \\ \hline .040 \end{array}$$

Example 4: Multiply .00785 by .25.

STEP 1: Write the numbers.

$$\begin{array}{r} .00785 \\ \times\ .25 \\ \hline \end{array}$$

STEP 2: Multiply the numbers as you would whole numbers.

$$\begin{array}{r} .00785 \\ \times\ .25 \\ \hline 3925 \\ 1570 \\ \hline 19625 \end{array}$$

STEP 3: Place the decimal point in the product.

Since .00785 is a five-place decimal and .25 is a two-place decimal, the total number of decimal places in the numbers being multiplied is seven. Therefore, the number of decimal places in the product must equal seven. Counting seven decimal places from right to left, the product becomes .0019625. Note that two zeros must be inserted to create the seven-place decimal.

$$\begin{array}{r} .00785 \\ \times\ .25 \\ \hline 3925 \\ 1570 \\ \hline .0019625 \end{array}$$

MULTIPLYING MIXED DECIMALS

Mixed decimals are multiplied in the same manner as decimal numbers.

Example 1: Multiply 4.65 by .75.

STEP 1: Write the numbers.

$$\begin{array}{r} 4.65 \\ \times\ .75 \\ \hline \end{array}$$

STEP 2: Multiply the numbers as you would whole numbers.

$$
\begin{array}{r}
4.65 \\
\times\ .75 \\
\hline
2325 \\
3255 \\
\hline
34875
\end{array}
$$

STEP 3: Place the decimal point in the product.

Since 4.65 has a two-place decimal and .75 is a two-place decimal, the total number of decimal places in the numbers being multiplied is four. Therefore, the number of decimal places in the product must equal four. Counting four decimal places from right to left, the product becomes 3.4875.

$$
\begin{array}{r}
4.65 \\
\times\ .75 \\
\hline
2325 \\
3255 \\
\hline
3.4875
\end{array}
$$

Example 2: Multiply 15.375 by 6.75.

STEP 1: Write the numbers.

$$
\begin{array}{r}
15.375 \\
\times\ 6.75
\end{array}
$$

STEP 2: Multiply the numbers as you would whole numbers.

$$
\begin{array}{r}
15.375 \\
\times\ 6.75 \\
\hline
76875 \\
107625 \\
92250 \\
\hline
10378125
\end{array}
$$

STEP 3: Place the decimal point in the product.

Since 15.375 has a three-place decimal and 6.75 has a two-place decimal, the total number of decimal places in the numbers being multiplied is five. Therefore, the number of decimal places in the product must equal five. Counting five decimal places from right to left, the product becomes 103.78125.

$$
\begin{array}{r}
15.375 \\
\times\ 6.75 \\
\hline
76875 \\
107625 \\
92250 \\
\hline
103.78125
\end{array}
$$

DIVIDING DECIMALS

Decimal numbers are divided in the same way that whole numbers are divided.

To determine the correct location of the decimal point in the quotient, move the divisor decimal point to the right as many places as are needed to make the divisor a whole number, then move the dividend decimal point to the right the same number of places. Place the decimal point in the quotient directly above the new location of the dividend decimal point. Here are some examples.

Example 1: Divide .15 by .3.

STEP 1: Write the problem.

$$.3\overline{)\,.15}$$

STEP 2: Move the divisor decimal point to the right as many places as are needed to make the divisor a whole number.

To make the divisor (.3) a whole number, move the decimal one place to the right. The result is the whole number 3.

$$3.\overline{)\,.15}$$

STEP 3: Move the dividend decimal point to the right the same number of places that you moved the divisor decimal point.

Since the divisor decimal point was moved one place to the right, you must move the dividend (.15) decimal point one place to the right. The result is the number 1.5.

$$3.\overline{)\,1.5}$$

STEP 4: Place the decimal point in the quotient.

$$3.\overline{)\,\overset{.}{1.5}}$$

STEP 5: Divide the numbers.

$$3.\overline{)\,\overset{.5}{1.5}}$$
$$\underline{1\ 5}$$
$$0$$

Therefore, $.15 \div .3 = .5$.

Example 2: Divide .75 by .25.

STEP 1: Write the problem.

$$.25\overline{)\,.75}$$

STEP 2: Move the divisor decimal point to the right as many places as are needed to make the divisor a whole number.

To make the divisor (.25) a whole number, move the decimal two places to the right. The result is the whole number 25.

$$25.\overline{)\,.75}$$

STEP 3: Move the dividend decimal point to the right the same number of places that you moved the divisor decimal point.

Since the divisor decimal point was moved two places to the right, you must move the dividend (.75) decimal point two places to the right. The result is the number 75.

$$25.\overline{)75.}$$

STEP 4: Place the decimal point in the quotient.

$$25.\overline{)75.}^{\,\cdot}$$

STEP 5: Divide the numbers.

$$
\begin{array}{r}
3. \\
25.\overline{)75.} \\
\underline{75} \\
0
\end{array}
$$

Therefore, .75 ÷ .25 = 3.

Example 3: Divide .64 by .004.

STEP 1: Write the problem.

$$.004\overline{)\,.64}$$

STEP 2: Move the divisor decimal point to the right as many places as are needed to make the divisor a whole number.

To make the divisor (.004) a whole number, move the decimal three places to the right. The result is the whole number 4.

$$4.\overline{)\,.64}$$

STEP 3: Move the dividend decimal point to the right the same number of places that you moved the divisor decimal point.

Since the divisor decimal point was moved three places to the right, you must move the dividend (.64) decimal point three places to the right. The result is the number 640. Note that it is necessary to add a zero in order to move the decimal three places.

$$4.\overline{)640.}$$

STEP 4: Place the decimal point in the quotient.

$$4.\overline{)640.}^{\,\cdot}$$

STEP 5: Divide the numbers.

$$
\begin{array}{r}
160. \\
4.\overline{)640.} \\
\underline{4} \\
24 \\
\underline{24} \\
0
\end{array}
$$

Therefore, .64 ÷ .004 = 160.

WHEN DECIMALS WON'T DIVIDE EVENLY

Not all decimals divide evenly. When division results in a quotient and a remainder, simply round off the quotient to an acceptable place value. Here is an example.

Example: Divide .38 by .6.

STEP 1: Write the problem.

$$.6)\overline{.38}$$

STEP 2: Move the divisor decimal point to the right as many places as are needed to make the divisor a whole number.

To make the divisor (.6) a whole number, move the decimal one place to the right. The result is the whole number 6.

$$6.)\overline{.38}$$

STEP 3: Move the dividend decimal point to the right the same number of places that you moved the divisor decimal point.

Since the divisor decimal point was moved one place to the right, you must move the dividend (.38) decimal point one place to the right. The result is the number 3.8.

$$6.)\overline{3.8}$$

STEP 4: Place the decimal point in the quotient.

$$6.)\overline{3.8}$$

STEP 5: Divide the numbers.

```
        .63333
   6.) 3.80000
       3 6
         20
         18
         20
         18
         20
         18
         20
         18
          2
```

Since the number does not divide evenly, round the number to an acceptable place value. A two-place decimal is acceptable for most woodworking, so the number becomes .63. Therefore, $.38 \div .6 = .63$.

DIVIDING MIXED DECIMALS

A mixed decimal is divided in the same manner as a decimal fraction is divided.

Example 1: Divide 3.5 by .875.

STEP 1: Write the problem.

$$.875\overline{)3.5}$$

STEP 2: Move the divisor decimal point to the right as many places as are needed to make the divisor a whole number.

To make the divisor (.875) a whole number, move the decimal three places to the right. The result is the whole number 875.

$$875.\overline{)3.5}$$

STEP 3: Move the dividend decimal point to the right the same number of places that you moved the divisor decimal point.

Since the divisor decimal point was moved three places to the right, you must move the dividend (3.5) decimal point three places to the right. The result is the number 3500. Note that it is necessary to add two zeros in order to move the decimal three places.

$$875.\overline{)3500.}$$

STEP 4: Place the decimal point in the quotient.

$$875.\overline{)3500.}^{\,\cdot}$$

STEP 5: Divide the numbers.

$$
\begin{array}{r}
4. \\
875.\overline{)3500.} \\
\underline{3500} \\
0
\end{array}
$$

Therefore, 3.5 ÷ .875 = 4.

Example 2: Divide .24 by 6.

STEP 1: Write the problem.

$$6\overline{).24}$$

STEP 2: Move the divisor decimal point to the right as many places as are needed to make the divisor a whole number.

Since the divisor already is a whole number, there is no need to move the decimal point.

STEP 3: Move the dividend decimal point to the right the same number of places that you moved the divisor decimal point.

Since the divisor decimal point was not moved, you don't need to move the dividend decimal point.

STEP 4: Place the decimal point in the quotient.

$$6\overline{)\overset{.}{}.24}$$

STEP 5: Divide the numbers.

$$6\overline{\smash{)}.24}$$
$$\begin{array}{r}.04\\[-2pt]\underline{24}\\0\end{array}$$

Therefore, .24 ÷ 6 = .04. Note that a zero is used in the quotient as a placeholder.

Example 3: Divide 194.6875 by 22.25.

STEP 1: Write the problem.

$$22.25\overline{\smash{)}194.6875}$$

STEP 2: Move the divisor decimal point to the right as many places as are needed to make the divisor a whole number.

To make the divisor (22.25) a whole number, move the decimal two places to the right. The result is the whole number 2225.

$$2225.\overline{\smash{)}194.6875}$$

STEP 3: Move the dividend decimal point to the right the same number of places that you moved the divisor decimal point.

Since the divisor decimal point was moved two places to the right, you must move the dividend (194.6875) decimal point two places to the right. The result is the number 19468.75.

$$2225.\overline{\smash{)}19468.75}$$

STEP 4: Place the decimal point in the quotient.

$$2225.\overline{)\overset{.}{}19468.75}$$

STEP 5: Divide the numbers.

$$2225.\overline{\smash{)}19468.75}$$
$$\begin{array}{r}8.75\\[-2pt]\underline{17800}\\16687\\[-2pt]\underline{15575}\\11125\\[-2pt]\underline{11125}\\0\end{array}$$

Therefore, 194.6875 ÷ 22.25 = 8.75.

CHANGING A FRACTION TO A DECIMAL

Changing a fraction into a decimal is easy: You simply divide the numerator of the fraction by the denominator. (To see how to change a decimal into a fraction, refer to chapter three.)

Example 1: Change $\frac{1}{4}$ into a decimal.

STEP 1: Write the problem, dividing the numerator by the denominator.

$$4\overline{)1}$$

STEP 2: Add a decimal point after the numerator (the dividend).

$$4\overline{)1.}$$

STEP 3: Add zeros as needed. (You can add more zeros as you divide the numbers, if necessary.)

$$4\overline{)1.00}$$

STEP 4: Place the decimal point in the quotient.

$$4\overline{)1.00}^{\,.}$$

STEP 5: Divide the numbers.

$$
\begin{array}{r}
.25 \\
4\overline{)1.00} \\
\underline{8} \\
20 \\
\underline{20} \\
0
\end{array}
$$

Therefore, $\frac{1}{4} = .25$.

Example 2: Change $\frac{23}{32}$ into a decimal.

STEP 1: Write the problem, dividing the numerator by the denominator.

$$32\overline{)23}$$

STEP 2: Add a decimal point after the numerator (the dividend).

$$32\overline{)23.}$$

STEP 3: Add zeros as needed.

$$32\overline{)23.00000}$$

STEP 4: Place the decimal point in the quotient.

$$32\overline{)23.00000}^{\,.}$$

STEP 5: Divide the numbers.

$$
\begin{array}{r}
.71875 \\
32\overline{)23.00000} \\
\underline{22\ 4} \\
60 \\
\underline{32} \\
280 \\
\underline{256} \\
240 \\
\underline{224} \\
160 \\
\underline{160} \\
0
\end{array}
$$

Therefore, $\frac{23}{32}$ = .71875, or .72 (rounded off to two decimal places).

WOODSHOP APPLICATION
Working With Decimals

A chart shows that 1×10 lumber contains .84 board feet of lumber for each lineal foot. If you need 65 board feet of 1×10 lumber for a project, how many lineal feet of the lumber must you buy?

Divide 65 board feet by .84 to find how many lineal feet of 1×10 lumber are needed.

$$.84\overline{)65}$$

Move the decimal points and divide.

$$
\begin{array}{r}
77.38 \\
84.\overline{)6500.00} \\
\underline{588} \\
620 \\
\underline{588} \\
320 \\
\underline{252} \\
680 \\
\underline{672} \\
8
\end{array}
$$

You'll need about $77\frac{1}{2}$ lineal feet of 1×10 lumber to yield 65 board feet.

CHAPTER 5

Powers and Roots

Some woodworkers might say an understanding of powers and roots is of little practical value in the woodshop. I suspect, however, that such skeptics would be surprised to learn that squares, square roots, cube roots and the like are often encountered when sawdust is flying. Indeed, a number of the formulas found in chapter seven (Plane Figure Formulas), chapter eight (Solid Figure Formulas) and chapter fourteen (Applying Handy Woodshop Formulas) incorporate the principles of powers and roots. A table of powers and roots for fractions from $\frac{1}{64}$ to $\frac{63}{64}$ and whole numbers from 1 to 100 can be found in the appendix.

UNDERSTANDING POWERS
Numbers multiplied together to form a product are called **factors**. For example, in the equation $2 \times 4 = 8$, the factors are 2 and 4. In $5 \times 1 \times 3 = 15$, the factors are 5, 1 and 3.

In arithmetic, a factor is sometimes repeatedly multiplied, for example, 3×3, or $7 \times 7 \times 7$ or $14 \times 14 \times 14 \times 14$. When a factor is repeatedly multiplied, the product that results is called a **power**. Therefore, 9 is the power of 3×3 (since $3 \times 3 = 9$), 343 is the power of $7 \times 7 \times 7$ (since $7 \times 7 \times 7 = 343$) and 38,416 is the power of $14 \times 14 \times 14 \times 14$ (since $14 \times 14 \times 14 \times 14 = 38,416$).

The factor that is repeatedly multiplied is called the **base**. The above examples have bases of 3, 7 and 14, respectively.

EXPONENTS
Repeatedly writing the base number to show repeated multiplication can get cumbersome. For example, to multiply the factor 2 by itself eight times you must write $2 \times 2 \times 2 \times 2 \times 2 \times 2 \times 2 \times 2$. In order to avoid having to write such long chains of numbers, we instead use a form of shorthand called an **exponent**. An exponent, which is written as a small, raised number adjacent to the base number, represents the number of times a base number must be repeatedly multiplied. Therefore, to show that the factor 2 is to be multiplied by itself eight times, you simply write 2^8. This is read as 2 to the eighth power. Here are a few other examples of exponents.

Example 1: Find the value of 9^4.
$$9^4 = 9 \times 9 \times 9 \times 9 = 6561$$

Note that for 9 to the fourth power, the base is 9, the exponent is 4 and the power is 6561.

Example 2: Find the value of 5^5.
$$5^5 = 5 \times 5 \times 5 \times 5 \times 5 = 3125$$

For 5 to the fifth power, the base is 5, the exponent is 5 and the power is 3125.

Example 3: What is the sixth power of 3?

$$3^6 = 3 \times 3 \times 3 \times 3 \times 3 \times 3 = 729$$

For 3 to the sixth power, the base is 3, the exponent is 6 and the power is 729.

Example 4: What is the value of 4^2?

$$4^2 = 4 \times 4 = 16$$

The base is 4, the exponent is 2 and the power is 16. This can be read as 4 to the second power, but the exponent ^{2} is commonly read as "squared." Therefore, read 4^2 as 4 squared.

Example 5: What is the value of 7^3?

$$7^3 = 7 \times 7 \times 7 = 343$$

The base is 7, the exponent is 3 and the power is 343. This can be read as 7 to the third power, but the exponent ^{3} is generally read as "cubed." Therefore, 7^3 is read as 7 cubed.

EXPONENTS WHEN THE BASE IS A FRACTION

When using exponents, the base number is not always going to be a whole number. It can sometimes be a fraction. Before you start fretting that a mix of exponents and fractions is sure to trigger a math-induced headache, you'll be relieved to know that the procedure is actually straightforward. Indeed, the procedure is much the same as the one used in chapter two to multiply fractions.

Keep in mind that when the base number is a fraction, it can be either a proper fraction or an improper fraction. The power of a proper fraction always has less value than the base number. Conversely, the power of an improper fraction always has greater value than the base number. Let's look at some examples.

Example 1: Find the value of $\left(\dfrac{2}{3}\right)^2$.

$$\left(\frac{2}{3}\right)^2 = \frac{2^2}{3^2} = \frac{2 \times 2}{3 \times 3} = \frac{4}{9}$$

Example 2: What is $\left(\dfrac{3}{4}\right)^4$?

$$\left(\frac{3}{4}\right)^4 = \frac{3^4}{4^4} = \frac{3 \times 3 \times 3 \times 3}{4 \times 4 \times 4 \times 4} = \frac{81}{256}$$

Example 3: Find the value of $\left(\dfrac{5}{2}\right)^3$.

$$\left(\frac{5}{2}\right)^3 = \frac{5^3}{2^3} = \frac{5 \times 5 \times 5}{2 \times 2 \times 2} = \frac{125}{8}$$

If desired, the improper fraction $\frac{125}{8}$ can be converted to the proper fraction $15\frac{5}{8}$.

EXPONENTS WHEN THE BASE IS A DECIMAL NUMBER

Not only can a base number be a whole number or a fraction, it can also be a decimal number. When the base is a decimal number, the procedure is much the same as the one used to multiply decimals in chapter four. To raise a decimal number to a power, you simply multiply the decimal number by itself as any times as indicated by the exponent. Here are some examples.

Example 1: What is the value of .25³?

$$.25^3 = .25 \times .25 \times .25 = .015625$$

Example 2: Find the value of .5².

$$.5^2 = .5 \times .5 = .25$$

Example 3: What is .375⁵?

$$.375^5 = .375 \times .375 \times .375 \times .375 \times .375 = .0074157$$

Example 4: What is the value of 4.27²?

$$4.27^2 = 4.27 \times 4.27 = 18.2329$$

DETERMINING THE POWER OF A POWER

You might, on occasion, come across a formula that requires you to find the power of a power. Let's work through some examples to show you how it's done.

Example 1: Find the value of (4²)³.

$$(4^2)^3 = (4 \times 4)^3$$
$$= 16^3$$
$$= 16 \times 16 \times 16$$
$$= 4096$$

Optional Method

You can also find the value by first multiplying the two exponents to determine a new exponent. Then, using the new exponent, raise the base number to its power. Here's how it works.

$$(4^2)^3 = 4^{2 \times 3} = 4^6$$
$$= 4 \times 4 \times 4 \times 4 \times 4 \times 4$$
$$= 4096$$

Example 2: Find the value of $(2.5^2)^2$.

$$(2.5^2)^2 = (2.5 \times 2.5)^2$$
$$= (6.25)^2$$
$$= 6.25 \times 6.25$$
$$= 39.0625$$

Optional Method

$$(2.5^2)^2 = 2.5^{2 \times 2} = 2.5^4$$
$$= 2.5 \times 2.5 \times 2.5 \times 2.5$$
$$= 39.0625$$

MULTIPLYING LIKE BASES: A SHORTCUT

When two or more like bases are to be multiplied, you can use this shortcut to save time and effort. Simply add the exponents to determine a new exponent. Then, using the new exponent, raise the common base number to its power. Here's how to do it. (Remember, this shortcut can only be used when you have like bases.)

Example 1: Multiply 5^2 by 5^3.

$$5^2 \times 5^3 = 5^{2+3}$$
$$= 5^5$$
$$= 5 \times 5 \times 5 \times 5 \times 5$$
$$= 3125$$

Example 2: Multiply 3^2 by 3^2 by 3^3.

$$3^2 \times 3^2 \times 3^3 = 3^{2+2+3}$$
$$= 3^7$$
$$= 3 \times 3 \times 3 \times 3 \times 3 \times 3 \times 3$$
$$= 2187$$

Example 3: Multiply $7^4 \times 3^2$.

Since the bases are unlike numbers (7 and 3), you can't use the shortcut. Instead, you must determine each power, then do the multiplication.

$$7^4 \times 3^2 = (7 \times 7 \times 7 \times 7) \times (3 \times 3)$$
$$= 2401 \times 9$$
$$= 21,609$$

DIVIDING LIKE BASES: A SHORTCUT

This shortcut can save you time and effort when two like bases are to be divided. First, determine a new exponent by subtracting the exponent of the divisor from the exponent of the dividend. Then, using the new exponent, raise the common base number to its power. Let's look at a couple of examples. (Remember, unlike bases cannot be divided using this shortcut.)

Example 1: Divide 6^5 by 6^3.

$$6^5 \div 6^3 = 6^{5-3}$$
$$= 6^2$$
$$= 36$$

Example 2: Divide 1.5^8 by 1.5^5.

$$1.5^8 \div 1.5^5 = 1.5^{8-5}$$
$$= 1.5^3$$
$$= 3.375$$

Example 3: Divide 5^4 by 2^3.

The bases are unlike numbers (5 and 2), so you can't use the shortcut. Instead, you must determine each power, then do the necessary division.

$$5^4 \div 2^3 = (5 \times 5 \times 5 \times 5) \div (2 \times 2 \times 2)$$
$$= 625 \div 8$$
$$= 78.125$$

UNDERSTANDING ROOTS

The **root** of any number can be defined as a factor that, when repeatedly multiplied, produces the number. For example, a root of 81 is 3, since the factor 3, when repeatedly multiplied, produces 81 ($3 \times 3 \times 3 \times 3 = 81$). A root of 3125 is 5, since the factor 5, when repeatedly multiplied, will yield 3125 ($5 \times 5 \times 5 \times 5 \times 5 = 3125$).

SQUARE ROOT

The **square root** of a number is a factor that when multiplied twice produces the number. For example, the square root of 9 is 3, since the factors 3 multiplied twice produces 9 ($3 \times 3 = 9$). The square root of 16 is 4, since $4 \times 4 = 16$.

CUBE ROOT

The **cube root** of a number is a factor that when multiplied three times produces the number. For example, the cube root of 8 is 2, since the factors 2 multiplied three times produces 8 ($2 \times 2 \times 2 = 8$). The cube root of 216 is 6, since $6 \times 6 \times 6 = 216$.

THE RADICAL SIGN

A special symbol ($\sqrt{}$) called a **radical sign** is used to indicate the root of a number. A small, raised number to the left of the radical sign, called an **index**, indicates how many times the equal factors are multiplied to produce the number. Therefore, $\sqrt[3]{25}$ indicates the cube root of 125, and $\sqrt[4]{81}$ indicates the fourth root of 81. A radical sign without an index number represents the square root of the number. For example, $\sqrt{64}$ means the square root of 64, and $\sqrt{100}$ indicates the square root of 100.

ROOTS AS FRACTIONS OR DECIMALS

Up to this point, all the roots we've looked at have been nice, round whole numbers. However, as you might expect, arithmetic is rarely this perfect. Indeed, the roots of most numbers include fractions or decimals. For example, the cube root of 6 ($\sqrt[3]{6}$) is 1.81712 and the square root of 8 ($\sqrt{8}$) is 2.82843. However, beyond the fact that roots with fraction and decimals have a few more digits, the basic procedure for using them remains the same.

FINDING THE ROOTS OF A NUMBER

You will recall from earlier in this chapter that you use an exponent and a base number in order to find the power of a number. The procedure for finding the root of a number is the reverse process. Here, since the power is known, you use an exponent and the power to find the root. There are several ways to determine the roots of a number. Let's look at the ones most commonly used.

FINDING ROOTS BY ESTIMATING

You can find the root of a number by doing a series of estimates. This procedure can be a bit slow, but it eventually gets the job done. Here are a couple examples.

Example 1: Find $\sqrt{34}$.

Start by making a guess. Pick a number that, when squared, will be close to 34. Let's choose 5.

$$5 \times 5 = 25$$

Too small, so try 6.

$$6 \times 6 = 36$$

Too big. Try 5.5, a number midway between 5 and 6.

$$5.5 \times 5.5 = 30.25$$

Too small. Try 5.8.

$$5.8 \times 5.8 = 33.64$$

Still too small, but getting close. Try 5.85.

$$5.85 \times 5.85 = 34.2225$$

A little too big, try 5.83.

$$5.83 \times 5.83 = 33.9889$$

The root is still a bit small, but it should be close enough for any woodworking application. Therefore, $\sqrt{34} = 5.83$.

Example 2: Find $\sqrt[4]{128}$.
Start by making a guess. Let's say 3.

$$3 \times 3 \times 3 \times 3 = 81$$

Too small, so try 4.

$$4 \times 4 \times 4 \times 4 = 256$$

Too big. Try 3.5, a number midway between 3 and 4.

$$3.5 \times 3.5 \times 3.5 \times 3.5 = 150.0625$$

Too big. Try 3.3.

$$3.3 \times 3.3 \times 3.3 \times 3.3 = 118.5921$$

A little small, but getting close. Try 3.36.

$$3.36 \times 3.36 \times 3.36 \times 3.36 = 127.45506$$

This is likely to be close enough for any woodworking application, but if you want it a bit closer, try 3.364.

$$3.364 \times 3.364 \times 3.364 \times 3.364 = 128.06308$$

That's pretty darn close—no need to go further. Therefore, $\sqrt[4]{128} = 3.364$.

FINDING ROOTS BY USING A TABLE
Most good math books include a table that lists the square and cube roots of many numbers. Indeed, a table with square and cube roots appears in the appendix of this book. Clearly, such a table will get you a root much faster than using the estimating method, as long as the number you are working with is listed in the table.

Example 1: Find the cube root of 51 ($\sqrt[3]{51}$).
Referring to the table in the appendix, the cube root of 51 is 3.70843.

Example 2: What is the square root of $\frac{9}{32}$ ($\sqrt{\frac{9}{32}}$)?
Referring to the table in the appendix, the square root of $\frac{9}{32}$ is .530330.

FINDING ROOTS BY USING A CALCULATOR
Most calculators on the market today—even the most basic types—have a square root key that enables you to quickly find the square root of a number. Simply punch in the number and hit the square root key. The number displayed is the square root.

Example: Find the square root of 257 ($\sqrt{257}$).
Using a calculator with a square root key, punch in the number 257 then hit the square root key. The number displayed, 16.031219, is the square root.

Specialized calculators, such as scientific calculators, also include keys that allow easy calculation of cube roots and other roots.

PART TWO

BASIC WOODSHOP GEOMETRY

CHAPTER 6
Common Geometric Shapes

In geometry, there are two basic types of shapes: those that have a **plane figure** and those that have a **solid figure**. Plane figures have length and width, but no depth. Examples include squares, rectangles, triangles, hexagons and circles. Solid figures have length, width *and* depth. Examples include prisms, cylinders, cones and spheres.

    This chapter will introduce some of the plane and solid figures that you might encounter in the woodshop. Once you can recognize the basic geometric shapes, you'll be able to do all sorts of useful things. For example, when you know that a tabletop you are building has a rectangular shape, it will be easy to calculate the surface area or the volume. Armed with that information, you will see in later chapters how to determine the number of board feet of stock needed or how much polyurethane you must to buy in order to apply three coats to all surfaces. You'll even be able to figure out, if need be, how much the top weighs.

PLANE FIGURES
Let's begin by looking at some of the plane geometric figures that you commonly find in the woodshop.

LINES
Since geometric figures are made up of lines, it's helpful to be able to recognize and name them.

Straight Line
The shortest distance between two points. (The term **line**, unless further defined, means a straight line.)

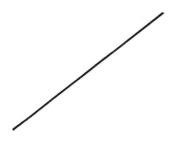

Horizontal Line
A line parallel to the horizon.

Vertical Line
A line perpendicular to the horizon.

Oblique Line
A line that is neither horizontal nor vertical.

Perpendicular Line
A line that intersects another line at 90°.

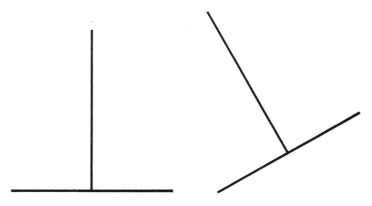

Parallel Lines
Two or more lines that remain the same distance apart at all points.

Irregular Curved Lines
A curved line with a radius that constantly changes.

ANGLES
When two lines meet, the space between them is called an **angle**. The two lines are called the **angle sides** and the point where they meet is called the **vertex**. An angle is usually measured in degrees. The various types of angles you're likely to come across in the woodshop are shown here.

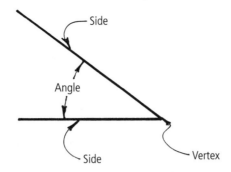

Straight Angle

Two lines that intersect to form a straight line. A straight angle measures 180°.

_____

Right Angle

The angle formed by a line perpendicular to another line. A ~~straight~~ *right* angle measures 90°.

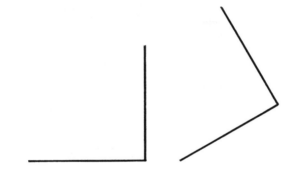

Acute Angle

An angle that is less than 90°.

Obtuse Angle
An angle that is more than 90° but less than 180°.

POLYGONS
A **polygon** is a closed plane figure that has three or more sides and angles. A polygon that has all angles equal and all sides equal in length is called a **regular polygon**. Polygons are usually named according to the number of sides they have. Some of the common polygons are:

Name	Number of Sides
Triangle	3
Quadrilateral	4
Pentagon	5
Hexagon	6
Octagon	8
Decagon	10
Dodecagon	12

Triangles
A polygon with three sides and three angles is called a **triangle**. It's not uncommon to come across triangle shapes in the woodshop. For example, bevels, tapers, wedges, dovetails and gussets, to name a few, all have triangular shapes.

Right Triangle
A triangle with one 90° angle.

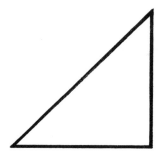

Equilateral Triangle
A triangle whose sides are of equal length.

Isosceles Triangle
A triangle with two sides of equal length.

Scalene Triangle
A triangle with all sides unequal in length.

Obtuse Triangle
A triangle with an obtuse angle.

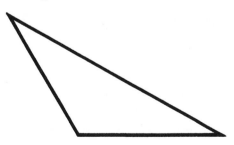

Quadrilaterals

A polygon with four sides and four angles is called a **quadrilateral**. In a quadrilateral, the sum of the four angles is always equal to 360°.

Quadrilaterals abound in the woodshop. You'll find that most tabletops have a square or rectangular shape. I've seen drafting tables with leg frames in the shape of a trapezoid. I once worked on an outdoor playhouse that had louvers cut to produce a rhomboid-shaped cross section.

Rectangle

A quadrilateral with four right angles.

Square

A quadrilateral with four right angles and four equal-length sides.

Rhomboid

A quadrilateral with opposite sides parallel, adjacent sides unequal, and usually having two acute angles and two obtuse angles.

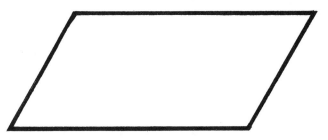

Rhombus
A quadrilateral with all sides equal in length, opposite sides parallel, and usually having two acute angles and two obtuse angles.

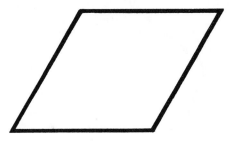

Trapezoid
A quadrilateral with two sides parallel and two sides not parallel.

Trapezium
A quadrilateral having no sides parallel.

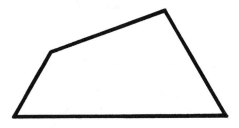

Other Polygons
Several other polygon shapes seem to regularly show up in the woodshop. Many old-time schoolhouse clocks are made using an octagon shape for the frame. Tabletops are sometimes made in the shape of a pentagon. I once built a display pedestal with a base that was shaped like a hexagon.

Regular Pentagon

A figure having five equal-length sides and five equal angles.

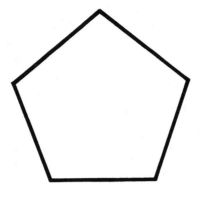

Regular Hexagon

A figure having six equal-length sides and six equal angles.

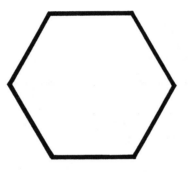

Regular Octagon

A figure having eight equal-length sides and eight equal angles.

Regular Decagon
A figure having ten equal-length sides and ten equal angles.

Regular Dodecagon
A figure having twelve equal-length sides and twelve equal angles.

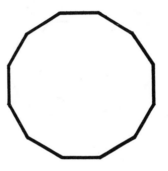

CIRCLES
All the shapes we have looked at so far have sides constructed from straight lines. But the circle is also an important part of geometry. Indeed, in the woodshop, circles are used to construct tabletops, toy wheels, clockfaces, round mirrors and much more. Of course, you'll see a circle when you look at a drilled hole or the end of any dowel, round table leg or lathe turning. Let's consider the circle and some of its related components.

Circle
A closed curve with all points of equal distance from the center point.

Concentric Circles

Two or more circles with the same center point but with different diameters.

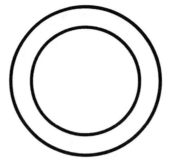

Eccentric Circles

Two or more circles with different center points.

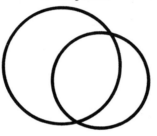

Semicircle

A half of a circle.

Circumference

The distance around a circle.

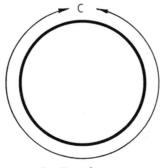

C = Circumference

Arc

A portion of the circumference.

Radius

A straight line extending from the center of a circle to any point on the circle.

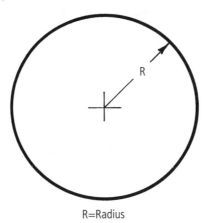

R=Radius

Diameter

A straight line that passes through the center of a circle and extends from one side of the circle to the other.

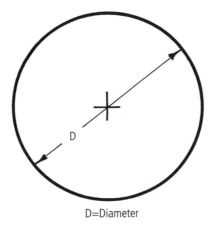

D=Diameter

Chord

A straight line connecting two points on a circle.

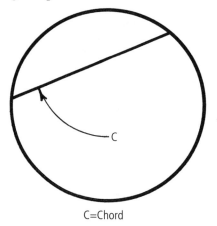

C=Chord

Tangent

A straight line that touches a circle at only one point.

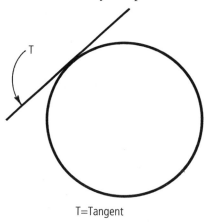

T=Tangent

Segment

That part of a circle (or any geometric figure) cut off by a straight line.

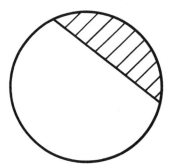

ELLIPSES

Dining tables are sometimes cut into the shape of an **ellipse**. The oval-shaped curve adds an interesting shape to the top and allows for comfortable seating around the table.

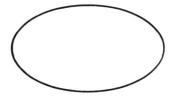

SOLID FIGURES

Here are some of the solid geometric figures you'll commonly find in the woodshop. In some cases, I'm afraid the definitions are almost painful to read, but I felt it best to include them anyway. Although you might not remember the definitions, I suspect you'll find the illustrations quickly clear up any confusion.

PRISMS

A **prism** is a solid with two parallel bases that are identical polygons. The prism ends are called **bases**, while the prism sides are called the **lateral faces**. A prism can be square, rectangular, triangular, pentagonal, and so on, according to the shape of the base.

Right Square Prism

A prism with lateral faces perpendicular to square bases.

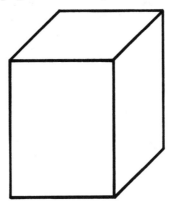

Cube or Hexahedron

A prism with bases and lateral faces that are squares.

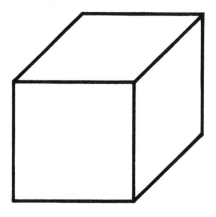

Right Rectangular Prism

A prism with lateral faces perpendicular to rectangular bases.

Oblique Rectangular Prism

A prism with lateral faces not perpendicular to rectangular bases.

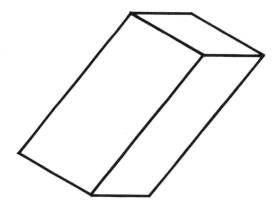

Triangular Prism

A prism with triangular bases.

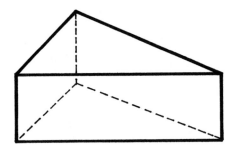

CYLINDERS

Strictly defined, a **cylinder** is a solid bounded by two equal, parallel circles and by a curved surface formed by moving a straight line of fixed length so the ends lie on the two parallel circles. Ouch! If a more palatable definition seems in order, let's simply say a cylinder has a shape like a can of soup.

Right Cylinder

A cylinder with the axis perpendicular to the bases. (The axis is the central line of any symmetrical or nearly symmetrical body.)

Oblique Cylinder

A cylinder with the axis not perpendicular to the base.

CONES

A **cone** is a solid with a circular base and a surface that narrows to a point at the top.

Right Cone

A cone whose axis is perpendicular to the base.

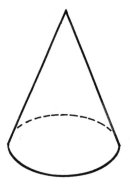

Oblique Cone

A cone whose axis is not perpendicular to the base.

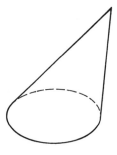

Truncated Right Cone
The portion remaining after a cutting plane is passed through a right cone.

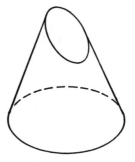

PYRAMIDS
A solid with a polygon for its base and triangles for its sides is called a **pyramid**.

Right Square Pyramid
A pyramid whose axis is perpendicular to a square base.

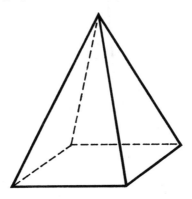

Oblique Square Pyramid
A pyramid whose axis is not perpendicular to a square base.

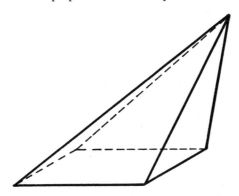

Right Rectangular Pyramid

A pyramid whose axis is perpendicular to a rectangular base.

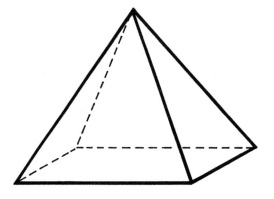

Right Triangular Pyramid

A pyramid whose axis is perpendicular to a triangular base.

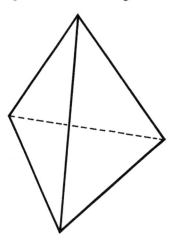

Truncated Pyramid

The portion remaining after a cutting plane is passed through a pyramid.

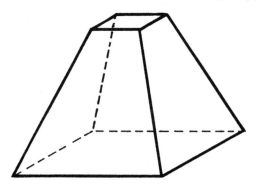

SPHERE

A **sphere** is a round solid figure in which every point on the surface is the same distance from the center. A baseball is a sphere.

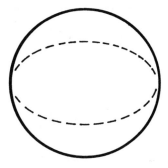

CHAPTER 7
Plane Figure Formulas

Plane figures, you will recall from chapter six, have length and width, but no depth. This chapter provides formulas for calculating both the area and the distance around each of the plane figures introduced in chapter six.

The amount of surface that a shape has is called its **area** or **surface area**. Square units of measurement (square inches, square feet, square millimeters, square meters, etc.) are used to describe area.

The distance around any closed plane figure is called the **perimeter**, while the distance around a circle is commonly called the **circumference**. Perimeter and circumference are described using linear units of measurement (inches, feet, millimeters, centimeters, and the like).

Triangle

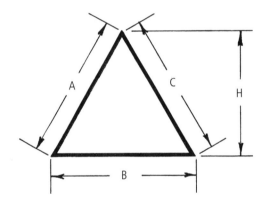

Area $= \frac{1}{2} B \times H$
Perimeter $= A + B + C$
where:
H = height of the triangle

Square

Area = S^2
Perimeter = $4 \times S$

Rectangle

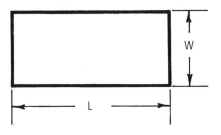

Area = $L \times W$
Perimeter = $(2 \times L) + (2 \times W)$

Rhomboid

Area = $B \times H$
where:
H = height of the rhomboid
Perimeter = $(2 \times A) + (2 \times B)$

Rhombus

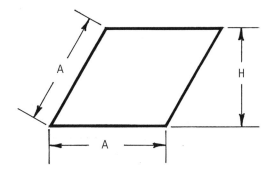

Area = A × H
where:
H = height of the rhombus
Perimeter = 4 × A

Trapezoid

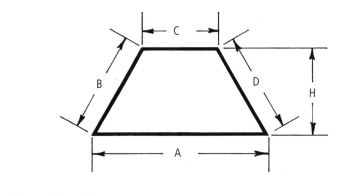

Area $= \dfrac{(A + C) \times H}{2}$

Perimeter = A + B + C + D

Trapezium

Area = $\dfrac{[(H + I) \times F] + (E \times H) + (G \times I)}{2}$

Perimeter = $A + B + C + D$

Regular Pentagon

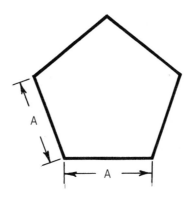

Area = $1.7205 \times A^2$

Perimeter = $5 \times A$

Regular Hexagon

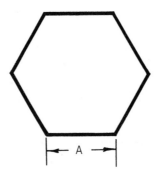

Area $= 2.5981 \times A^2$
Perimeter $= 6 \times A$

Regular Octagon

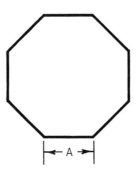

Area $= 4.8284 \times A^2$
Perimeter $= 8 \times A$

Regular Decagon

Area $= 7.6924 \times A^2$
Perimeter $= 10 \times A$

Regular Dodecagon

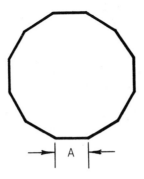

Area = 11.1961 × A²
Perimeter = 12 × A

Ellipse

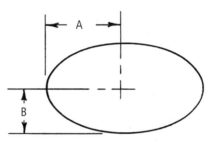

Area = 3.14159 × A × B
Perimeter (approximate) = 3.14159 [1.5(A + B) − $\sqrt{A \times B}$]

Circle

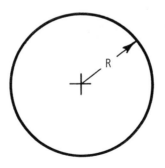

Area = 3.14159 × R²
where:
R = radius of the circle
Circumference = 6.2832 × R

WOODSHOP APPLICATION
Using the Area Formula

A woodshop floor measuring 15′ by 20′ is to be covered with pine flooring. According to the flooring supplier, 1.38 board feet of pine is needed for each square foot of floor. How many board feet of flooring must be ordered?

STEP 1: Calculate the area of the floor in square feet. Since the floor has the shape of a rectangle, use the formula for the area of a rectangle.

Area = L × W

Area = 20′ × 15′

Area = 300 square feet

STEP 2: Multiply the area of the floor (in square feet) by 1.38 to determine how many board feet of flooring are needed.

$$300 \times 1.38 = 414 \text{ board feet}$$

WOODSHOP APPLICATION
Using the Perimeter Formula

A tabletop made from $\frac{3}{4}''$ thick walnut plywood measures 48″ by 48″. The plywood requires an edging made from $\frac{3}{4}''$ by $\frac{3}{4}''$ walnut stock. The ends of the edging are mitered. How many feet of edging are needed?

STEP 1: Calculate the perimeter of the tabletop. Since the tabletop has the shape of a square, use the formula for the perimeter of a square.

Perimeter = 4 × S

Perimeter = 4 × 48″

Perimeter = 192″

STEP 2: Convert inches to feet (see conversion table in appendix).

$$192'' \times .08333 = 16'$$

CHAPTER 8
Solid Figure Formulas

From chapter six, you know that a solid figure has three dimensions: length, width and depth. Two important measurements of a solid figure are its volume and surface area. **Volume** is a measure of the three-dimensional size of a solid figure. **Surface area**, you will recall from chapter seven, is a measure of the amount of surface on the figure.

This chapter provides formulas for calculating the volume and surface area for several of the solid figures shown in chapter six. Volume is measured in cubic units (cubic inches, cubic feet, cubic millimeters, cubic meters, etc.). Surface area is measured in square units (square inches, square feet, square millimeters, square meters, etc.).

Cube (also called a Hexahedron)

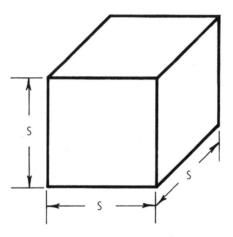

Volume $= S^3$
Surface Area $= 6 \times S^2$
where:
$S =$ side length

Right Rectangular Prism

Volume = L × W × H
Surface Area = 2(L × W) + 2(W × H) + 2(L × H)
where:
L = prism length
W = prism width
H = prism height

Right Cylinder

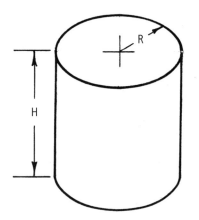

Volume = 3.14159 × R^2 × H
Surface Area = (6.28318 × R) × (R + H)
where:
R = radius of cylinder
H = height of cylinder

Right Cone

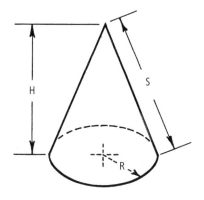

Volume $= \dfrac{3.14159 \times R^2 \times H}{3}$

Surface Area $= 3.14159 \times R \times (R + S)$

where:

R = radius of base

H = height of cone

S = length of side

Note: H is perpendicular to the base.

Right Square Pyramid

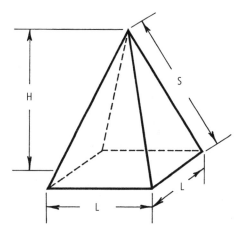

Volume $= \dfrac{L^2 \times H}{3}$

Surface Area $= (2 \times L \times S) + L^2$

where:

L = base length

H = height of pyramid

S = side length

Note: H is perpendicular to the base.

Right Rectangular Pyramid

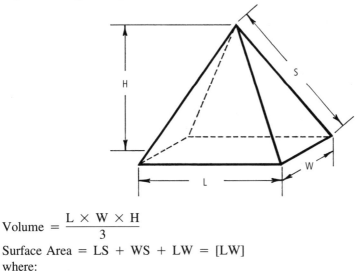

$$\text{Volume} = \frac{L \times W \times H}{3}$$

Surface Area = LS + WS + LW = [LW]

where:

L = base length

W = base width

H = height of pyramid

S = side length

Note: H is perpendicular to the base.

Right Pyramid (General Formula)

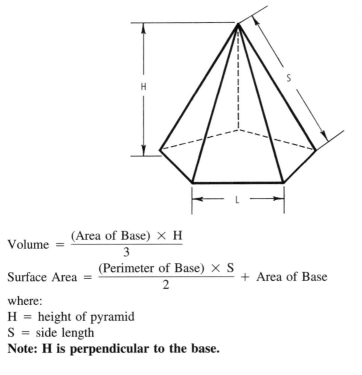

$$\text{Volume} = \frac{(\text{Area of Base}) \times H}{3}$$

$$\text{Surface Area} = \frac{(\text{Perimeter of Base}) \times S}{2} + \text{Area of Base}$$

where:

H = height of pyramid

S = side length

Note: H is perpendicular to the base.

Sphere

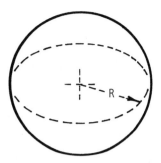

Volume $= 4.1888 \times R^3$
Surface Area $= 12.5664 \times R^2$
where:
R $=$ radius of sphere

WOODSHOP APPLICATION
Using the Surface Area Formula

The top of a dining table measures $1\frac{1}{2}''$ thick by 3' wide by 7' long. The top requires three coats of varnish. How much varnish is needed if it covers at a rate of 100 square feet per quart?

STEP 1: Determine the surface area of the tabletop (in square feet). Since the tabletop has the shape of a right rectangular prism, use the formula:

Surface Area $= 2(L \times W) + 2(W \times H) + 2(L \times H)$

L $=$ length $= 7'$

W $=$ width $= 3'$

H $=$ height $= 1\frac{1}{2}''$

STEP 2: Convert the $1\frac{1}{2}''$ height (H) to feet (see conversion tables in appendix) so all the dimensions have the same unit of measurement.

$$H = 1\frac{1}{2}'' \times .08333 = .125''$$

STEP 3: Calculate the surface area using the formula.

Surface Area = 2(L × W) + 2(W × H) + 2(L × H)

Surface Area = 2(7 × 3) + 2(3 × .125) + 2(7 × .125)

Surface Area = 2(21) + 2(.375) + 2(.875)

Surface Area = 42 + .75 + 1.75

Surface Area = 44.5 square feet

STEP 4: Determine the total surface area to be covered by 3 coats of varnish.

3 coats × 44.5 square feet = 133.5 square feet

Since the varnish covers at a rate of 100 square feet per quart, you'll need just under $1\frac{1}{2}$ quarts (133.5 ÷ 100 = 1.335) to complete the job.

CHAPTER 9

Basic Geometric Construction

In the woodshop, it's often helpful to be able to quickly sketch a portion of a project or even a wood joint. The various geometric construction techniques shown here can save you time and effort whenever a quick sketch is in order. You'll find they can be done with a minimum of tools. Indeed, for most of the constructions, you'll need only a couple of drafting triangles, a straightedge and a compass.

In this chapter you'll also find that you can use geometric constructions to create some interesting patterns that are perfect for inlaying, chip carving or decorating painted furniture. Several of the patterns shown are commonly used to decorate furniture in the Pennsylvania Dutch style.

Finally, this chapter shows you how to quickly create a number of different angles using only a couple of drafting triangles and a T square.

THE BASIC CONSTRUCTIONS STEP BY STEP

I've always enjoyed working with drafting tools, so I find it fun to do these constructions. It's also the best way to get familiar with them, so sharpen the pencil point on your compass, collect some scrap paper and go to work.

BISECTING A STRAIGHT LINE

To **bisect** a straight line is to divide the line in half. Either a compass or a drafting triangle can be used for this.

Compass Method

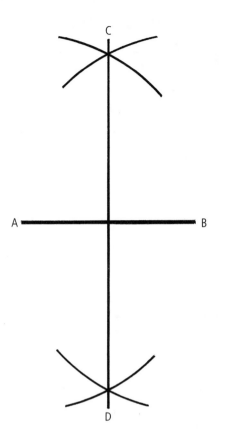

STEP 1: Set the compass for any radius greater than the length of AB.

STEP 2: With points A and B as centers, use the compass to mark intersecting arcs at C and D.

STEP 3: Draw a straight line through CD to bisect the line AB.

Drafting Triangle Method

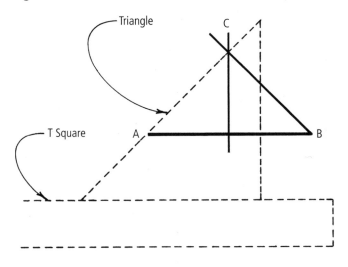

STEP 1: Tape paper to drafting board.

STEP 2: Use the T square to draw line AB.

STEP 3: With the T square and a 45° (or 60°) drafting triangle, draw lines through points A and B to create point C.

STEP 4: Draw a straight line perpendicular to AB through point C to bisect line AB.

TRISECTING A STRAIGHT LINE

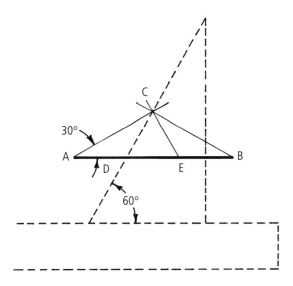

To **trisect** a straight line is to divide the line into thirds. You'll need the T square and a 30° × 60° drafting triangle to do the work.

STEP 1: Tape paper to drafting board.

STEP 2: Use the T square to draw line AB.

STEP 3: Draw two lines at 30°, one through point A and one through point B.

STEP 4: Mark the intersection of the two lines as point C.

STEP 5: Draw two lines at 60° through point C to line AB.

STEP 6: To complete the trisection, mark the intersection of the lines as points D and E. Line AD = line DE = line EB.

BISECTING AN ARC
To bisect an arc is to find the arc's midpoint.

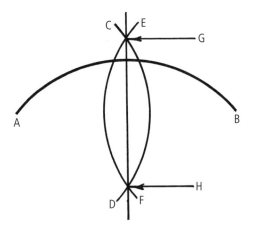

STEP 1: Set the compass for any radius greater than one-half the length of arc AB.

STEP 2: With point A as the center, scribe arc CD.

STEP 3: With point B as the center, scribe arc EF.

STEP 4: Mark the points of intersection of arcs CD and EF as G and H.

STEP 5: To complete the bisection, draw a straight line connecting points G and H.

BISECTING AN ANGLE

To bisect an angle is to divide the angle in half.

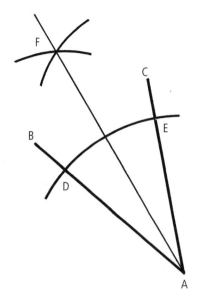

STEP 1: Label points A (the vertex), B and C on the angle.

STEP 2: With point A as the center, use the compass to scribe an arc that intersects the angle sides at D and E.

STEP 3: Set the compass for any radius greater than the length of chord DE.

STEP 4: Use the compass to scribe a pair of intersecting lines, one with point D as a center, one with point E as the center. Label the intersection as point F.

STEP 5: Draw line AF to bisect the angle.

DRAWING AN ANGLE EQUAL TO ANOTHER ANGLE

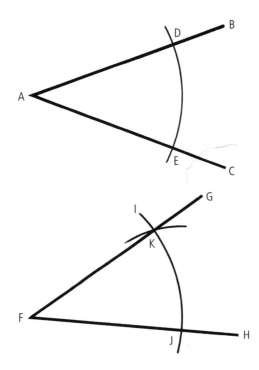

STEP 1: Label points A (the vertex), B and C on the angle.

STEP 2: Draw line FH to represent one side of the new angle.

STEP 3: With point A as the center, use the compass to scribe an arc that intersects the angle sides at D and E.

STEP 4: With the compass at the same radius, and with point F on the new triangle as the center, scribe a long arc that intersects line FH at J.

STEP 5: Set the compass to a radius that equals the length of chord DE.

STEP 6: With point J as the center, scribe an arc to intersect arc IJ at K.

STEP 7: Draw line FG through K to complete the angle.

DRAWING AN EQUILATERAL TRIANGLE

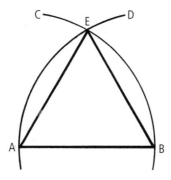

STEP 1: Draw line AB to represent the length of one side of the triangle.

STEP 2: Set the compass for a radius that equals the length of line AB.

STEP 3: With point A as the center, scribe the arc BC.

STEP 4: With point B as the center, scribe the arc AD.

STEP 5: Mark the point where the arcs intersect as E.

STEP 6: To complete the equilateral triangle, draw straight lines connecting AE and BE.

DRAWING A SQUARE WHEN GIVEN THE DIAGONAL

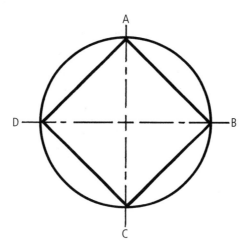

STEP 1: Using the compass, scribe a circle with a diameter that is equal to the length of the diagonal.

STEP 2: Extend two perpendicular center lines to the edge of the circle.

STEP 3: Mark the four points where the center lines intersect the circle as A, B, C and D.

STEP 4: To complete the square, draw a straight line connecting points AB, BC, CD and DA.

DRAWING A SQUARE WHEN GIVEN THE SIDE

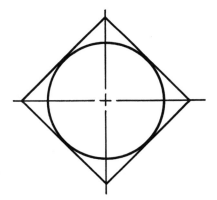

STEP 1: Use the compass to scribe a circle with a diameter that is equal to the length of the side.

STEP 2: Extend two perpendicular center lines to the edge of the circle.

STEP 3: Use a 45° triangle to draw four straight lines, each one tangent to the circle and at 45° to the center lines.

DRAWING A REGULAR PENTAGON

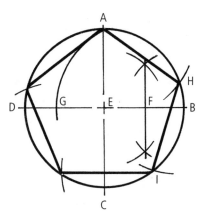

STEP 1: Use the compass to scribe a circle, then draw two perpendicular center lines.

STEP 2: Mark the four points where the centerlines intersect the circle as A, B, C and D.

STEP 3: Mark the center point of the circle as E.

STEP 4: Bisect the line EB. Mark the midpoint of line EB as F.

STEP 5: Set the compass for a radius that equals the length of FA.

STEP 6: Using point F as the center point, scribe the arc AG.

STEP 7: Set the compass for a radius that equals the length of AG.

STEP 8: Starting with point A as a center point, use the compass to scribe an arc that intersects the circle at H. Next, with point H as the center point, scribe an arc that intersects at I. Continue this procedure two more times to complete a total of five points on the circle.

STEP 9: To complete the pentagon, draw five straight lines to connect the five points on the circle.

DRAWING A REGULAR HEXAGON

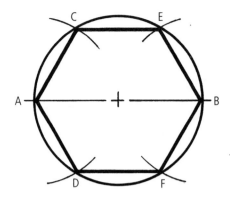

STEP 1: Use the compass to draw a circle.

STEP 2: Draw two perpendicular center lines and mark points A and B.

STEP 3: Without changing the compass setting, use point A as a center point to scribe arcs locating points C and D.

STEP 4: Using point B as a center point, scribe arcs to locate points E and F.

STEP 5: To complete the hexagon, draw six straight lines to connect the six points on the circle.

DRAWING A REGULAR OCTAGON

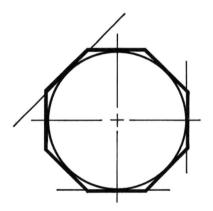

STEP 1: Use the compass to draw a circle, then draw two perpendicular center lines.

STEP 2: Use a 45° triangle to draw four straight lines, each one tangent to the circle and at 45° to the center lines.

STEP 3: Use a 90° triangle to draw two straight vertical lines tangent to the circle.

STEP 4: To complete the octagon, use the T square to draw two straight horizontal lines tangent to the circle.

DRAWING ANY REGULAR POLYGON

A decagon is used here as an example, but the same basic procedure can be applied to any regular polygon.

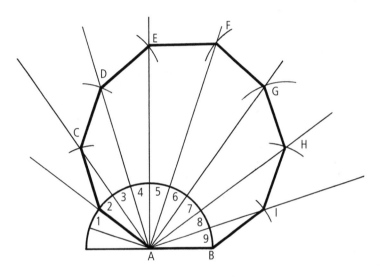

STEP 1: Draw line AB representing the length of one side of the polygon.

STEP 2: Set the compass for a radius that equals the length of AB.

STEP 3: With point A as a center point, draw a semicircle.

STEP 4: Divide the semicircle into equal parts. The number of equal parts must equal the number of polygon sides. For a decagon—a ten-sided polygon—the semicircle is divided into ten parts. A semicircle has 180°, so 180° ÷ 10 = 18° in each equal part. Use a protractor to mark points on the semicircle at 18°, 36°, 54°, 72°, 90°, 108°, 126°, 144° and 162°. Label the points 1 through 9, as shown.

STEP 5: Draw an extended straight line from point A through point 2. Do the same for points 3 through 9.

STEP 6: With the compass still set for a radius that equals the length of AB, use point 2 as a center point and scribe an arc to intersect line A3. Mark this point as C.

STEP 7: Use point C as a center point and scribe an arc to intersect line A4. Mark this point as D.

STEP 8: Use point D as a center point and scribe an arc to intersect line A5. Mark this point as E. (You can continue working your way around the polygon to complete the layout, but the construction is likely to be more accurate if the next step begins at point B.)

STEP 9: Use point B as a center point and scribe an arc to intersect line A9. Mark this point as I.

STEP 10: Use point I as a center point and scribe an arc to intersect line AB. Mark this point as H.

STEP 11: Use point H as a center point and scribe an arc to intersect line A7. Mark this point as G.

STEP 12: Use point G as a center point and scribe an arc to intersect line A6. Mark this point as F.

STEP 13: To complete the decagon, connect points A, 2, C, D, E, F, G, H, I and B.

DRAWING AN ARC TANGENT TO A RIGHT ANGLE

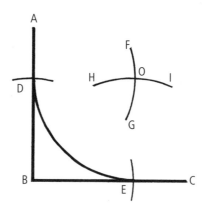

STEP 1: Draw line AB at a right angle to line BC.

STEP 2: Set the compass to equal the radius of the desired arc.

STEP 3: Use point B as a center point and scribe an arc that intersects lines AB and BC. Label the points of intersection as D and E.

STEP 4: With the same compass setting, use point D as a center point and scribe arc FG.

STEP 5: With the same compass setting, use point E as a center point and scribe arc HI. Mark the intersection of arcs FG and HI as O.

STEP 6: With the same compass setting, use point O as a center point and scribe the arc connecting points D and E. The arc is tangent to the right angle at D and E.

DRAWING AN ARC TANGENT TO AN ACUTE ANGLE

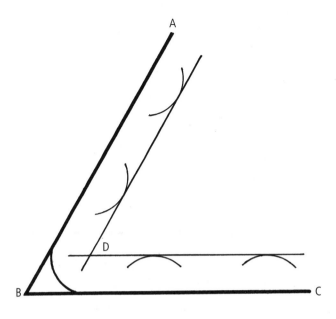

STEP 1: Draw line AB at an acute angle to line BC.

STEP 2: Set the compass to equal the radius of the desired arc.

STEP 3: Select a point near each end of lines AB and BC as center points, then scribe an arc at each point.

STEP 4: Draw lines tangent to the arcs.

STEP 5: Mark the intersection of the lines as point D.

STEP 6: Without changing the compass setting, use point D as a center point and scribe an arc connecting lines AB and BC. The arc is tangent to the acute angle formed by lines AB and BC.

DRAWING AN ARC TANGENT TO AN OBTUSE ANGLE

STEP 1: Draw line AB at an obtuse angle to line BC.

STEP 2: Set the compass to equal the radius of the desired arc.

STEP 3: Select a point near each end of lines AB and BC as center points, then scribe an arc at each point.

STEP 4: Draw lines tangent to the arcs.

STEP 5: Mark the intersection of the lines as point D.

STEP 6: Without changing the compass setting, use point D as a center point and scribe an arc connecting lines AB and BC. The arc is tangent to the obtuse angle formed by lines AB and BC.

DRAWING AN ELLIPSE

An ellipse can be drawn using any one of several geometric construction methods. The method used here, called the **trammel method**, is particularly useful when you want to draw a full-size ellipse.

STEP 1: Draw a horizontal line slightly longer than the ellipse length and the vertical line slightly longer than the ellipse width.

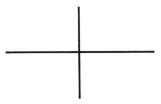

STEP 2: Mark points X, Y and Z on a straightedge made from cardboard, stiff paper or a thin piece of wood. Make the length of XY equal to one-half the ellipse width. Make the length of XZ equal to one-half the ellipse length.

STEP 3: Position the straightedge so that point Z falls at any point on the vertical line and point Y falls on the horizontal line. Hold the straightedge in position, then mark point X. The mark at point X represents a point on the perimeter of the ellipse.

STEP 4: Continue moving the straightedge, always keeping point Z on the vertical line and point Y on the horizontal line. Mark a new point X after each movement of the straightedge. Mark as many points as are needed to create a smooth curve along the entire perimeter of the ellipse.

CONSTRUCTING DECORATIVE PATTERNS STEP BY STEP

With a little know-how and a compass, you can easily create some interesting decorative patterns. All of these patterns can be put to good use on painted furniture. In addition, the heart-shaped pattern is often used as a decorative cutout on country furniture and accessories. Many chip carvers like to work with the five-point star and six-petal flower.

DRAWING A FIVE-POINT STAR

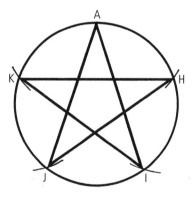

STEP 1: Follow steps 1 through 8 in "Drawing a Regular Pentagon" (page 103).

STEP 2: Mark the points on the circle as A, H, I, J and K.

STEP 3: Use a straight line to connect points AI, AJ, HK, HJ and IK.

DRAWING A FOUR-POINT STAR IN A SQUARE

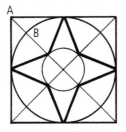

STEP 1: Draw a square.

STEP 2: Use straight lines to construct the diagonals.

STEP 3: With the intersection of the diagonals as a center point, scribe a circle tangent to the sides of the square.

STEP 4: Set the compass to equal length AB.

STEP 5: With the intersection of the diagonals as a center point, use the compass to scribe a second circle inside the square.

STEP 6: Connect the points of the star as shown.

DRAWING A SIX-PETAL FLOWER

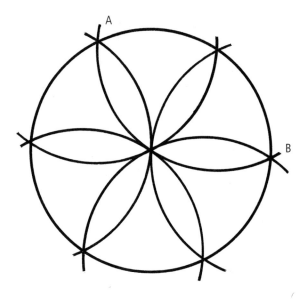

STEP 1: Set the compass to equal the radius of the flower.

STEP 2: Scribe the diameter.

STEP 3: Using any point on the diameter as a center point, scribe an arc that intersects the diameter at two points.

STEP 4: Mark the intersections of the diameter as points A and B.

STEP 5: With point A as a center point, use the same compass setting to scribe a second arc.

STEP 6: With point B as a center point, use the same compass setting to scribe a third arc.

STEP 7: Continue in this manner until the all six petals are scribed.

DRAWING A TRIANGLE IN A CIRCLE

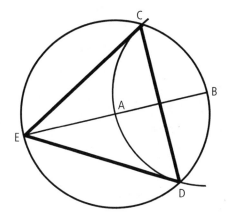

STEP 1: Set the compass to equal the radius of the desired diameter.

STEP 2: Scribe the diameter and mark the center point as A.

STEP 3: Select any point on the diameter and mark it as B.

STEP 4: With point B as the center point, use the same compass setting to scribe an arc. Mark the points that the arc intersects the diameter as C and D.

STEP 5: Use a straightedge to draw an extended line through points A and B. Mark the point that the line intersects the diameter as E.

STEP 6: To complete the triangle, use the straightedge to connect points C, D and E.

DRAWING A HEART

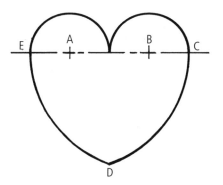

STEP 1: Use the compass to scribe two semicircles tangent to each other. Mark the center points as A and B.

STEP 2: Set the compass to equal the distance AC.

STEP 3: With point A as a center point, scribe arc CD.

STEP 4: To complete the heart, use point B as a center point and scribe arc ED.

ANGLES FROM TRIANGLES

Two triangles—a 45° and a 30° × 60°—when used in combination, can quickly create an assortment of commonly used angles.

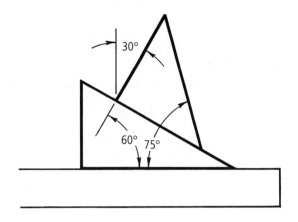

CHAPTER 10
Basic Geometric Theorems

In geometry, any statement or rule that can be proved to be true is called a **theorem**. An understanding of some of the basic theorems can often be helpful in the woodshop. Let's look at some of them.

When two lines intersect, the angles opposite each other are equal.

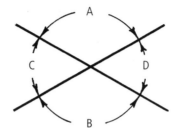

Angle A = Angle B
Angle C = Angle D

When a line intersects two parallel lines, the corresponding angles on each of the parallel lines are equal.

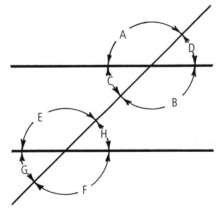

Angle A = Angle B = Angle E = Angle F
Angle C = Angle D = Angle G = Angle H

In any triangle, the sum of the three angles is 180°.

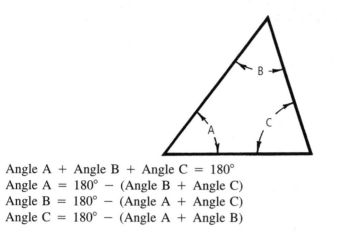

Angle A + Angle B + Angle C = 180°
Angle A = 180° − (Angle B + Angle C)
Angle B = 180° − (Angle A + Angle C)
Angle C = 180° − (Angle A + Angle B)

When a triangle has three sides equal in length (an equilateral triangle), the three angles are equal (60°).

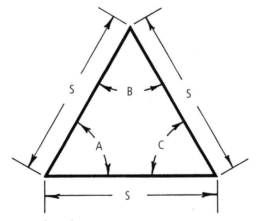

All sides (S) are the same length.
Therefore:
Angle A = Angle B = Angle C = 60°

When a triangle has three 60° angles, the sides are equal in length and the triangle is an equilateral triangle.

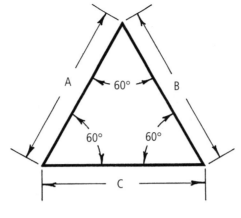

All angles are 60°.
Therefore:
Side A = Side B = Side C

When a triangle is equilateral, a line bisecting an angle also bisects the side opposite the angle. Also, the bisecting line is perpendicular to the side opposite the angle.

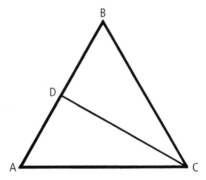

Line CD bisects Angle ACB
Therefore:
Line AD = Line BD
Line CD is perpendicular to Line AB

When a triangle has two sides that are equal in length (an isosceles triangle), the angles opposite the two equal-length sides are also equal.

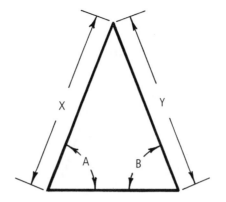

Side X = Side Y
Therefore:
Angle A = Angle B

When a triangle has two angles that are equal, the sides opposite the two equal angles are equal in length.

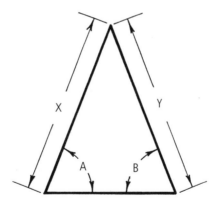

Angle A = Angle B
Therefore:
Side X = Side Y

When a triangle is isosceles, a line bisecting the angle formed by the intersection of the two equal-length sides bisects the side opposite that angle. Also, the bisecting line is perpendicular to the side opposite the angle.

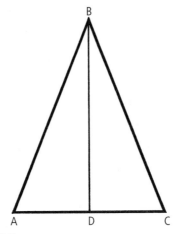

Line BD bisects Angle ABC
Therefore:
Line AD = Line DC
Line BD is perpendicular to Line AC

In any triangle, the exterior angle of a side is equal to the sum of the two opposite interior angles. (The exterior angle is the angle between a side of a triangle and a line extended from the adjacent side.)

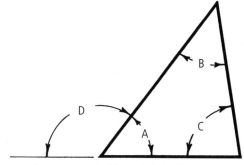

Angle D (the exterior angle) = Angle B + Angle C

In any quadrilateral (four-sided figure), the sum of the four angles is 360 °.

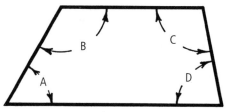

Angle A + Angle B + Angle C + Angle D = 360°
The equation can also be written as:
Angle A = 360° − (Angle B + Angle C + Angle D)
Angle B = 360° − (Angle A + Angle C + Angle D)
Angle C = 360° − (Angle A + Angle B + Angle D)
Angle D = 360° − (Angle A + Angle B + Angle C)

WOODSHOP APPLICATION
Using a Geometric Theorem

One end of a 1×8 pine board is square cut; the other is cut at a 58° angle. What is the angle of B?

STEP 1: Recognize that the beveled board has the shape of a quadrilateral.

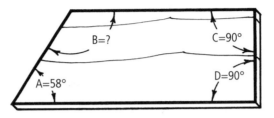

STEP 2: Since the square cut end produces a pair of 90° angles, the known angles of the board are 58°, 90° and 90°. Label the known angles A, C and D respectively.

STEP 3: Apply the formula:

Angle B = 360 − (Angle A + Angle C + Angle D)

Angle B = 360 − (58 + 90 + 90)

Angle B = 360 − 238

Angle B = 122°

PART THREE

USING MATH IN THE WORKSHOP

CHAPTER 11

ENLARGING GRID PATTERNS

Unlike an arc, which has a constant radius, an irregular curve, as defined in chapter six, is a curve with a constantly changing radius. Woodworking projects often include parts with irregular curves. Such curves add interesting shapes to parts like bracket feet, table legs, aprons, stretchers, decorative scrollwork designs, toy parts and more.

However, when working from a plan in a woodworking book or magazine, project parts with irregular curves can be a bit problematic. Because books and magazines are relatively small in size, full-size curved parts can't usually be shown. Also, irregular curves can't be accurately defined using the length, width and depth dimensions used to detail the size and shape of most parts.

To solve this problem, books and magazines usually add a grid pattern to irregularly curved parts. A grid pattern allows book and magazine editors to present irregular curves in a reduced size, yet the grid provides all the information needed for the reader to enlarge the curve to full size.

Short of buying a pantograph, a grid pattern can be enlarged to full size in a couple ways. The **grid square method** is the one most commonly used, although, as photocopiers become more common, the **photocopy method** is gaining favor with many woodworkers. This chapter shows you how to do both.

THE GRID SQUARE METHOD

Many woodworkers quickly become glassy-eyed when faced with using the grid square method to enlarge a pattern. Perhaps it's a suspicion that one must be blessed with artistic talent in order to do an enlargement. Believe me—and this comes from someone who has trouble drawing straight lines with a good ruler—nothing can be further from the truth. This procedure is pretty straightforward, and once you understand it, you'll no longer find yourself squaring the corners of a gracefully curved bracket foot in order to avoid the procedure altogether.

Let's look at an example and work it through step-by-step.

STEP 1: Determine the grid scale.

Find the scale, which can usually be found in an area adjacent to the grid pattern. Commonly used scales are: 1 square $= \frac{1}{2}''$; 1 square $= \frac{3}{4}''$; 1 square $= 1''$ (the most common scale); 1 square $= 1\frac{1}{2}''$ and 1 square $= 2''$. Our example uses a scale of 1 square $= 1''$.

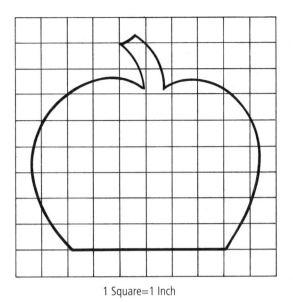

1 Square=1 Inch

STEP 2: Number the squares on the grid pattern.

Working from a common corner, number each of the grid lines in both a horizontal and vertical direction.

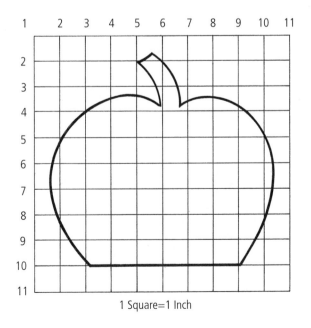

1 Square=1 Inch

STEP 3: Lay out a full-size grid.

On a clean piece of paper, use a ruler to scribe horizontal and vertical lines corresponding to the number of lines used on the grid pattern. The distance between each line is determined by the grid scale—1″ in our example.

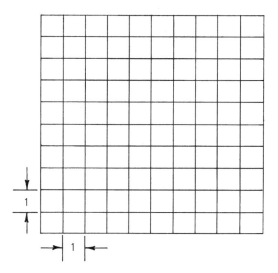

STEP 4: Number the lines on the full-size grid.

Working from the same common corner established in step 2, number the horizontal and vertical lines to correspond with those on the grid pattern.

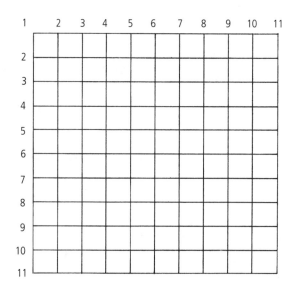

STEP 5: Mark the corresponding points of intersection.

Looking at the grid pattern, note where the curved pattern intersects with a grid line. Find the corresponding point of intersection on the full-size grid and mark that point with a dot. Continue this procedure, adding dots at each corresponding point of intersection between the curved pattern and the grid lines. The numbered lines, which serve as guides, will help minimize confusion. When completed, the full-size grid will look much like a connect-the-dots pattern.

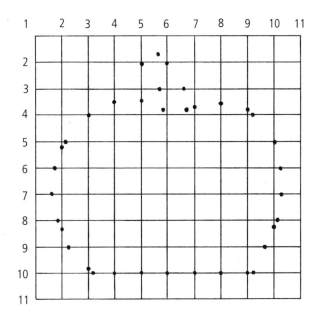

STEP 6: Connect the dots.

With the dots as a guide, you should be able to make a freehand sketch that's pretty close to the one on the grid pattern. If this isn't working to your satisfaction, use a french curve or a flexible curve to help with the job. Both of these drawing tools are sold at most art supply stores. Keep in mind that, in most cases, the full-size grid pattern doesn't have to be a perfect copy of the original pattern, so don't worry too much if the match isn't exact.

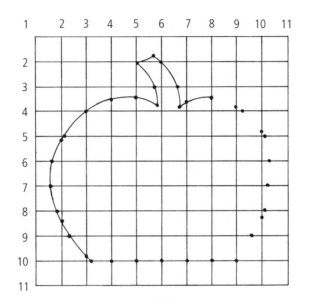

THE PHOTOCOPY METHOD

A photocopier can be a real time-saver when enlarging a grid pattern. Not only does a photocopier save time, you'll find that a pattern doesn't even require a grid in order to be enlarged—you simply work from the curved pattern as shown in the book or magazine.

The table shown here requires the use of a photocopier that can enlarge at least 150 percent. To find such a machine, check your local copy center. The enlargements are accurate to within 1 percent.

You'll need to determine the percentage of enlargement before you can use the table. To determine the percentage of enlargement:

1. Determine the desired full-size length of the pattern
2. Measure the length of the pattern on the grid
3. Divide the desired full-size length by the measured length of pattern on the grid, then multiply by 100

Example:

Plans for a hutch cupboard show a grid pattern for a curved bracket foot. The full-size curve must measure 6″ long. On the pattern, the curve measures $1\frac{7}{8}$″ inches long. How much must the curve be enlarged to produce a full-size pattern?

$$\text{percentage of enlargement} = \frac{\text{desired full-size length}}{\text{measured length of pattern on grid}} \times 100$$

$$= \frac{6}{1\frac{7}{8}} \times 100$$

$$= 3.2 \times 100$$

$$= 320 \text{ percent}$$

Once the percentage of enlargement is known, the table below details how to enlarge the pattern using a photocopier.

To enlarge original by: (percentage of enlargement)	Step 1 Photocopy original using a setting of:	Step 2 Photocopy first copy using a setting of:	Step 3 Photocopy second copy using a setting of:	Step 4 Photocopy third copy using a setting of:
percent	percent	percent	percent	percent
155	150	103	---	---
160	150	107	---	---
165	150	110	---	---
170	150	113	---	---
175	150	117	---	---
180	150	120	---	---
185	150	123	---	---
190	150	127	---	---
195	150	130	---	---
200	150	133	---	---
205	150	137	---	---
210	150	140	---	---
215	150	143	---	---
220	150	147	---	---
225	150	150	---	---
230	150	150	102	---
235	150	150	104	---
240	150	150	107	---
245	150	150	109	---
250	150	150	111	---
255	150	150	113	---
260	150	150	116	---
265	150	150	118	---
270	150	150	120	---
275	150	150	122	---
280	150	150	124	---

To enlarge original by: (percentage of enlargement)	Step 1 Photocopy original using a setting of:	Step 2 Photocopy first copy using a setting of:	Step 3 Photocopy second copy using a setting of:	Step 4 Photocopy third copy using a setting of:
percent	percent	percent	percent	percent
285	150	150	127	---
290	150	150	129	---
295	150	150	131	---
300	150	150	133	---
305	150	150	136	---
310	150	150	138	---
315	150	150	140	---
320	150	150	142	---
325	150	150	144	---
330	150	150	147	---
335	150	150	149	---
340	150	150	150	101
345	150	150	150	102
350	150	150	150	104
355	150	150	150	105
360	150	150	150	107
365	150	150	150	108
370	150	150	148	111
375	150	150	150	111
380	150	150	148	114
385	150	150	150	114
390	150	150	148	117
395	150	150	150	117
400	150	150	148	120

CHAPTER 12
Simplifying Compound Angles

A **compound angle** is created when a workpiece is cut at an angle using a saw blade that is also tilted at an angle (Fig. 12-1). The compound angle is commonly used to create taper-sided boxes and containers. The taper (tilt) angle of the box side is measured from a vertical line (Fig. 12-2). Compound angles can be cut on the table saw or the radial arm saw. Keep in mind, however, that saw gauges are notoriously inaccurate, so it's always best to make test cuts on scrap stock.

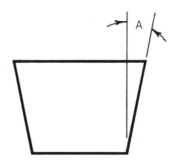

Fig. 12-2

The saw blade angle (Fig. 12-3) is measured from a vertical line for both the table saw and radial-arm saw. The angle of the table saw miter gauge (Fig. 12-4) is measured from a line perpendicular to the saw blade. The angle of the radial arm saw (Fig. 12-5) is measured from a line perpendicular to the fence.

Not all manufacturers use the same points of reference when establishing the blade tilt and cutting angles shown on their saw gauges. Therefore, the angles marked on your saw gauge might not correspond with the angles shown in the table. To avoid confusion, always set the saw based on angles B and C in Figures 12-3, 12-4 and 12-5.

A = tilt angle of sides

B = blade angle of table saw or radial arm saw

C = angle of table saw miter gauge or radial arm saw

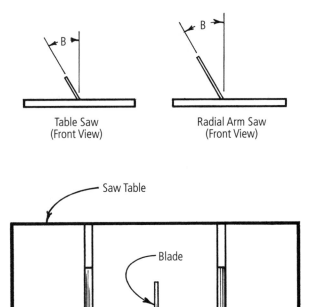

Table Saw
(Front View)

Radial Arm Saw
(Front View)

Fig. 12-3

Saw Table

Blade

C   C

Top View

Fig. 12-4

Top View

Fig. 12-5

Four-Sided Figure	A (degrees)	B (degrees)	C (degrees)
	5	44.8	4.9
	10	44.1	9.9
	15	43.1	14.5
	20	41.6	18.9
	25	39.9	22.9
	30	37.8	26.6
	35	35.4	29.8
	40	32.8	32.7
	45	30.0	35.3
	50	27.0	37.5
	55	23.9	39.3
	60	20.7	40.9

Five-Sided Figure	A (degrees)	B (degrees)	C (degrees)
	5	35.8	3.6
	10	35.4	7.2
	15	34.6	10.7
	20	33.6	14.0
	25	32.2	17.1
	30	30.6	20.0
	35	28.8	22.6
	40	26.8	25.0
	45	24.6	27.2
	50	22.2	29.1
	55	19.7	30.8
	60	17.1	32.2

Six-Sided Figure	A (degrees)	B (degrees)	C (degrees)
	5	29.9	2.9
	10	29.5	5.7
	15	28.9	8.5
	20	28.0	11.2
	25	27.0	13.7
	30	25.7	16.1
	35	24.2	18.3
	40	22.5	20.4
	45	20.7	22.2
	50	18.8	23.9
	55	16.7	25.3
	60	14.5	26.6

Eight-Sided Figure	A (degrees)	B (degrees)	C (degrees)
	5	22.4	2.1
	10	22.1	4.1
	15	21.7	6.1
	20	21.1	8.1
	25	20.3	9.9
	30	19.4	11.7
	35	18.3	13.4
	40	17.1	14.9
	45	15.7	16.3
	50	14.2	17.6
	55	12.7	18.7
	60	11.0	19.7

Ten-Sided Figure	A (degrees)	B (degrees)	C (degrees)
	5	17.9	1.6
	10	17.7	3.2
	15	17.4	4.8
	20	16.9	6.3
	25	16.3	7.8
	30	15.5	9.2
	35	14.7	10.6
	40	13.7	11.8
	45	12.6	12.9
	50	11.5	14.0
	55	10.2	14.9
	60	8.9	15.7

Twelve-Sided Figure	A (degrees)	B (degrees)	C (degrees)
	5	14.9	1.3
	10	14.8	2.7
	15	14.5	4.0
	20	14.1	5.2
	25	13.6	6.5
	30	13.0	7.6
	35	12.2	8.7
	40	11.4	9.8
	45	10.6	10.7
	50	9.6	11.6
	55	8.5	12.4
	60	7.4	13.1

WOODSHOP APPLICATION
Cutting Compound Angles

Using your table saw, you want to build a four-sided flatware tray that has a tilt angle of 20°. What table saw settings are going to produce the correct compound miter angle?

STEP 1: Find the table for four-sided figures.

STEP 2: Find the row for a tilt angle (A) of 20°.

STEP 3: Read across the row to find a table saw blade angle (B) of 41.6° and a miter gauge angle (C) of 18.9°.

CHAPTER 13
Solving Right Triangles

From chapter six, you will recall that a **right triangle** has one 90° angle (Fig. 13-1). Right triangles are found in many woodworking designs. For example, a miter becomes a right triangle simply by scribing a line perpendicular to the edge of the board (Fig. 13-2), as does a dovetail (Fig. 13-3). The back of an early American hooded cradle includes four right triangles (Fig. 13-4).

A right triangle has a **hypotenuse**, a fancy word meaning the side opposite the right angle. The hypotenuse is always the longest side of the triangle. The remaining two sides of the triangle are called the **legs**. Sometimes, the horizontal leg is called the *base*, and the vertical leg is called the **side**. The intersection of the two legs forms the right angle. In most drawings of a right triangle, a small box is added to designate that the angle shown is a right angle.

Fig. 13-1

Fig. 13-2

Fig. 13-3

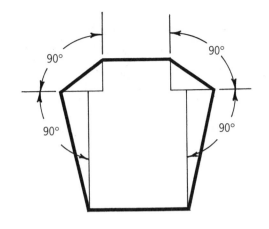

Fig. 13-4

Because we encounter right triangles with such regularity in the woodshop, it's useful to be able to calculate the lengths of the triangle sides and the angles they form. The process of doing these calculations is commonly referred to as "solving a right triangle." Once you can solve right triangles, you'll be surprised how often you practice the skill in the woodshop.

This chapter shows how to solve right triangles using either the Pythagorean theorem method or the table method. The Pythagorean theorem method detailed here enables you to determine the side lengths of a right triangle, while the table method shows how to determine not only the side lengths, but also the angles of a right triangle.

USING THE PYTHAGOREAN THEOREM

Pythagoras, a Greek philosopher, teacher and mathematician who lived around 500 B.C., is credited with proving that there is a proportional relationship between the sides of a right triangle. His theorem, which we now call the Pythagorean theorem, states that in any right triangle, the square of the hypotenuse is equal to the sum of the squares of the two other sides. Basically, this means that if you know the length of any two sides of a right triangle, you can determine the third side. Written as a formula, it looks like this:

$A^2 + B^2 = C^2$

A = the base

B = the side

C = the hypotenuse

The same formula can be written in several other useful forms:

$A = \sqrt{C^2 - B^2}$

$B = \sqrt{C^2 - A^2}$

$C = \sqrt{A^2 + B^2}$

Fig. 13-5

WOODSHOP APPLICATION
Using the Pythagorean Theorem to Solve a Right Triangle
(Solving for One Side When Two Sides Are Known)

Suppose you need to cut a right-angled gusset to serve as a stiffener for the back of a
case (Fig. 13-6). To fit in the available space, the gusset must measure 5″ diagonally
and have a base that's 4″ long. What is the length of the remaining side?

Fig. 13-6

STEP 1: Determine what is known about the right triangle.
As shown in Fig. 13-6, you know the following:

A = the base = 4″

B = the side = unknown

C = the hypotenuse = 5″

STEP 2: Determine if the known information allows you to solve the triangle. You
know the length of two sides of the right triangle (A and C), therefore you can solve
for the unknown side (B).

STEP 3: Select the equation that allows you to solve for the unknown. Use the equation
that solves for B:

$$B = \sqrt{C^2 - A^2}$$

STEP 4: Solve the equation:

$$B = \sqrt{5^2 - 4^2}$$

$$B = \sqrt{25 - 16}$$

$$B = \sqrt{9}$$

$$B = 3$$

The side is 3″ long.

USING TABLES

Using the formulas that follow, you can determine the unknown *sides* of a right triangle if you know one of the angles (other than the 90° angle) and the length of one side. You can also determine the unknown *angles* of a right triangle if you know the lengths of at least two of the sides.

In some cases it might be necessary to use two of the formulas to get the answer you need. The first formula solves for an unknown side or angle. Then, the new information is applied to a second formula that can provide the final answer. Of course, if you know two of the sides and want to know the third, you can also use the Pythagorean theorem as discussed earlier. However, when using the tables, note that the triangles are labeled differently than when using the Pythagorean theorem.

The reference angle (A) is the angle (other than the 90° angle) used to help solve the triangle (Fig. 13-7). It's important to keep in mind that when the location of the reference angle changes, the locations of sides B and C also change.

Finally, remember that the three angles in a triangle always equal 180°. If you know one of the angles (other than the 90° angle) you can get the unknown angle using the following formula:

$$\text{Unknown Angle} = 180 - (90 + \text{known angle}).$$

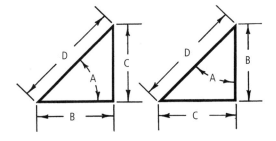

Fig. 13-7

A = reference angle (based on Angle Functions in Tables I, II or III)
B = side adjacent to the reference angle
C = side opposite the reference angle
D = side opposite the 90° angle (the hypotenuse)

Angle Functions
Tables

Angle (A) (in degrees)	I	II	III
0	.00000	1.00000	.00000
1	.01746	.99985	.01745
2	.03492	.99939	.03490
3	.05241	.99863	.05234
4	.06993	.99756	.06976
5	.08749	.99619	.08716
6	.10510	.99452	.10453
7	.12278	.99255	.12187
8	.14054	.99027	.13937
9	.15838	.98769	.15643
10	.17633	.98481	.17365
11	.19438	.98163	.19081
12	.21256	.97815	.20791
13	.23087	.97437	.22495
14	.24933	.97030	.24192
15	.26795	.96593	.25882
16	.28675	.96126	.27564
17	.30573	.95630	.29237
18	.32492	.95106	.30902
19	.34433	.94552	.32557
20	.36397	.93969	.34202
21	.38386	.93358	.35837
22	.40403	.92718	.37461
23	.42447	.92050	.39073
24	.44523	.91355	.40674
25	.46631	.90631	.42262
26	.48773	.89879	.43837
27	.50953	.89101	.45399
28	.53171	.88295	.46947
29	.55431	.87462	.48481
30	.57735	.86603	.50000
31	.60086	.85717	.51504
32	.62487	.84805	.52992
33	.64941	.83867	.54464
34	.67451	.82904	.55919
35	.70021	.81915	.57358
36	.72654	.80902	.58779
37	.75355	.79864	.60182
38	.78129	.78801	.61566
39	.80978	.77715	.62932
40	.83910	.76604	.64279
41	.86929	.75471	.65606
42	.90040	.74314	.66913
43	.93252	.73135	.68200
44	.96569	.71934	.69466
45	1.00000	.70711	.70711

Solving Right Triangles When One Side and One Angle Are Known

If you know the length of:	And you want to know the length of:	Use this formula:
B	C	$C = A \text{ (from Table I)} \times B$
B	D	$D = \dfrac{B}{A \text{ (from Table II)}}$
C	B	$B = \dfrac{C}{A \text{ (from Table I)}}$
C	D	$D = \dfrac{C}{A \text{ (from Table III)}}$
D	C	$C = A \text{ (from Table III)} \times D$
D	B	$B = A \text{ (from Table II)} \times D$

WOODSHOP APPLICATION
Using the Tables to Solve a Right Triangle (When One Side and One Angle Are Known)

A lap desk to be built must have sides that are 14″ long and have a 15° slant. If the front end of the sides measure 3″, what is the overall width of the sides?

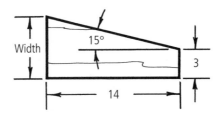

Fig. 13-8

The desk side creates a right triangle with one angle known (A) and one side known (B). To determine the overall width of a side, calculate the length of side C, then add that length to 3″.

Fig. 13-9

STEP 1: Determine what is known about the right triangle.
As shown in Fig. 13-9, you know the following:

A = the reference angle = 15°

B = the side adjacent to the reference angle = 14"

C = the side opposite the reference angle = unknown

STEP 2: Determine if the known information allows you to solve the triangle.
You know one angle (A) and the length of one side (B), therefore you can solve for the unknown side (C).

STEP 3: Select the equation that allows you to solve for the unknown.
Use the equation that solves for C when you know angle A and side B:

$$C = A \text{ (from Table I)} \times B$$

Step 4: Solve the equation:
Per Table I, an angle (A) of 15° has an angle function of .26795. Therefore:

$$C = .26795 \times 14$$
$$= 3.7513 \text{ (round to 3.75} = 3\tfrac{3}{4}")$$

Step 5: Add to determine the total width of the side.

$$\text{Width of side} = 3\tfrac{3}{4}" + 3"$$
$$= 6\tfrac{3}{4}"$$

Solving Right Triangles When Two Sides Are Known

If you know the length of:	And you know the length of:	Use this formula to find angle A:
B	C	$A \text{ (from Table I)} = \dfrac{C}{B}$
B	D	$A \text{ (from Table II)} = \dfrac{B}{D}$
C	D	$A \text{ (from Table III)} = \dfrac{C}{D}$

Once the angle function (A) is determined, use the appropriate table to find the corresponding angle.

WOODSHOP APPLICATION
Using the Tables to Solve a Right Triangle
(When Two Sides Are Known)

A coffee table is to have four 15″ long legs made from $1\frac{3}{4}$″ square stock. The legs are to be tapered on two sides, with each taper starting $4\frac{1}{4}$″ from the top of the leg. At the bottom of the leg, the taper reduces the thickness of the leg by $\frac{3}{4}$″. You need to determine the angle of the taper so that you can use a tapering jig to cut the tapers.

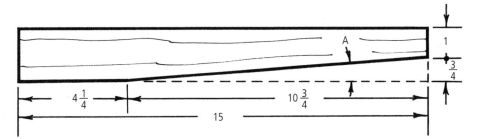

Fig. 13-10

STEP 1: Determine what is known about the right triangle.
As shown in Fig. 13-10, you know the following:

A = the reference angle = unknown

B = the side adjacent to the reference angle = $10\frac{3}{4}$ = 10.75

C = the side opposite the reference angle = $\frac{3}{4}$ = .75

STEP 2: Determine if the known information allows you to solve the triangle.
You know the length of two sides (B and C), therefore you can solve for the unknown angle (A).

STEP 3: Select the equation that allows you to solve for the unknown.
Use the equation that solves for angle A when you know sides B and C:

$$A \text{ (from Table I)} = \frac{C}{B}$$

Step 4: Solve the equation:

$$A \text{ (from Table I)} = \frac{C}{B}$$

$$= \frac{.75}{10.75}$$

$$= 0.06977$$

From Table I: An angle function of 0.06977 equals an angle of about 4°. Therefore, the angle of the taper (A) is 4°.

CHAPTER 14

Applying Handy Woodshop Formulas

An **equation** shows that two numbers or two groups of numbers equal the same amount. A **formula**, on the other hand, is an equation that shows a unique relationship between certain things. For example, when working with a triangular part, we know that the formula $A = \frac{1}{2}B \times H$ shows the unique relationship between certain things in a triangle, specifically the area (A), length of the base (B) and the height (H).

I prefer to define a formula in simpler terms. To me, a formula is simply a concise set of instructions for solving a particular problem. Indeed, a good formula, properly applied, can take a tough task and reduce it to a simple exercise in basic arithmetic.

This chapter provides a smorgasbord of easy-to-use formulas for use in the woodshop. Once you learn how to apply the formulas, you'll be able to solve an assortment of problems—from figuring the moisture content of wood to calculating the weight of a cherry tabletop.

DETERMINING WOOD MOISTURE CONTENT

A moisture meter is the fastest and easiest way to measure the moisture content in a piece of wood. Although moisture meters have become more affordable in recent years, most woodworkers feel the cost is still too high to justify the expense.

Without a moisture meter in hand, your other option is to calculate the moisture content of the wood. Although the procedure is very accurate, it isn't altogether practical for the average hobbyist woodworker. That's because you need a laboratory (gram) scale or an equivalent scale to get accurate weight measurements of the wood sample. Then, too, it can take up to 24 hours for the wood sample to fully dry in a kitchen oven—a procedure that's likely to disrupt any cooking schedule.

If, despite the drawbacks, you are still inclined to do this calculation, you'll need a wood sample that's about 1″ thick by 3″ wide by 1″ long (Fig. 14-1). Cutting the sample in this manner exposes a considerable amount of end grain, which helps the sample dry faster. Check to make sure that the sample doesn't have any knots or other defects. Also, avoid cutting the sample from the ends, which tend to be drier than other parts of the board.

Using the laboratory scale, weigh the sample and note the weight. Then place the sample in the oven and bake it at a temperature of 210° to 220° Fahrenheit. Reweigh the sample about every eight hours, taking care to avoid scorching the wood as it dries. When the sample no longer loses weight it is at the oven-dry weight, which means it is completely free of water and has a moisture content of zero. Once you have the oven-dry weight of the sample, you can determine the wood moisture content (MC) by using the following formula:

$$MC = \frac{\text{Original Weight} - \text{Oven-Dry Weight}}{\text{Oven-Dry Weight}} \times 100$$

Fig. 14-1

WOODSHOP APPLICATION
Determining Wood Moisture Content

The original weight of a sample is 14 grams. After completely drying in the oven, the sample weighs 12 grams. What is the moisture content of the sample?

$$MC = \frac{\text{Original Weight} - \text{Oven-Dry Weight}}{\text{Oven-Dry Weight}} \times 100$$

$$= \frac{14 \text{ grams} - 12 \text{ grams}}{12 \text{ grams}} \times 100$$

$$= \frac{2 \text{ grams}}{12 \text{ grams}} \times 100$$

$$= .167 \times 100$$

$$= 16.7 \text{ percent}$$

DETERMINING SIDE LENGTHS FOR POLYGONS

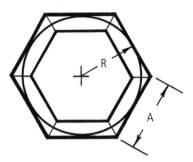

Fig. 14-2

For any figure with sides of equal length, use the following formula to calculate the lengths of the sides:

A = R × C

A = length of side

C = constant (see Constant Chart below)

R = radius of a circle that is tangent to the sides of the polygon

Constant Chart	
Number of Equal-Length Sides	**Constant**
3 (equilateral triangle)	3.464
4 (square)	2.000
5 (regular pentagon)	1.453
6 (regular hexagon)	1.155
8 (regular octagon)	0.828
10 (regular decagon)	0.650
12 (regular dodecagon)	0.536

WOODSHOP APPLICATION
Determining Side Lengths for a Polygon

You are preparing to build an octagonal wall clock that must be 16″ wide. What length do you cut each of the eight sides?

A 16″ wide clock has a radius of 8″.

The constant for a regular octagon is 0.828.

$$A = R \times C$$

$$= 8 \times 0.828$$

$$= 6.624″ \text{ inches (round to } 6\tfrac{5}{8}″)$$

Cut each side to a length of $6\tfrac{5}{8}″$.

MITER ANGLES FOR POLYGONS (WHEN ALL SIDES ARE EQUAL LENGTH)

The miter angles for several common polygons are shown. For polygons not shown, use the miter angle formula that follows to calculate the angle.

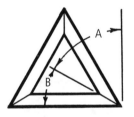

Equilateral Triangle
A = 60°
B = 30°

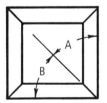

Square (also Rectangle)
A = 45°
B = 45°

Regular Pentagon
A = 36°
B = 54°

Regular Hexagon
A = 30°
B = 60°

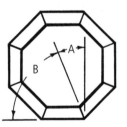

Regular Octagon
A = $22\frac{1}{2}°$
B = $67\frac{1}{2}°$

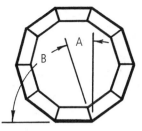

Regular Decagon
A = 18°
B = 72°

Regular Dodecagon
A = 15°
B = 75°

MITER ANGLE FORMULA

For any figure with sides of equal length, use the following formula to calculate the miter angle (A):

$$A = \frac{180}{N}$$

A = the miter angle (measured from vertical)

N = the number of sides

WOODSHOP APPLICATION

Using the Miter Angle Formula

You are building a box with nine equal sides. What is the miter angle for each of the sides?

$$A = \frac{180}{N}$$

$$A = \frac{180}{9}$$

$$A = 20°$$

ARC FORMULAS

Use these formulas to calculate the dimensions of an arc.

$$L = 2\sqrt{H(2R - H)}$$

$$R = \frac{L^2 + 4H^2}{8H}$$

$$H = R - \left(\frac{\sqrt{4R^2 - L^2}}{2}\right)$$

where:

L = the arc length
H = the arc height
R = the arc radius

WOODSHOP APPLICATION

Using the Arc Formulas

The ends of a bench require an arc-shaped cutout that measures 3″ high and 12″ inches long. What is the radius (R) of the arc?

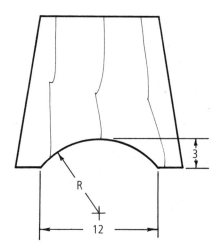

STEP 1: Since the height and length of the arc are known, you can use the formula that solves for the arc radius:

$$R = \frac{L^2 + 4H^2}{8H}$$

STEP 2: Plug in the knowns and solve the formula

$$R = \frac{12^2 + (4 \times 3^2)}{(8 \times 3)}$$

$$R = \frac{144 + 36}{24}$$

$$R = \frac{180}{24}$$

$$R = 7.5$$

The arc has a radius of $7\frac{1}{2}''$.

PARTICLEBOARD SHELF-SPAN FORMULAS

Particleboard is a common shelving material. Typically, shelves are exposed to two types of loads: uniform and concentrated. A uniform load is applied across the entire length of a shelf, for example, a shelf filled with books. On the other hand, a concentrated load is applied to a relatively small area of a shelf. A belt sander sitting in the middle of an otherwise empty shelf is an example of a concentrated load.

Use this chart to determine the maximum uniform and concentrated loads for various lengths and thicknesses of grade M-2 particleboard. The chart offers five thickness options: $\frac{1}{2}''$, $\frac{5}{8}''$, $\frac{3}{4}''$, $1''$ and $1\frac{1}{8}''$. The chart also shows the maximum deflection (sag) when the given shelf length is at maximum uniform load.

The chart data is based on using end supports that are securely anchored in place and extend across the full width of the shelf.

Span (Length)

UNIFORM LOADS

For uniform loads, use the following formula:

$$\text{Uniform load} = \frac{\text{expected load on the shelf (in pounds)}}{\text{area of shelf (in square feet)}}$$

WOODSHOP APPLICATION
Calculating Uniform Load on a Particleboard Bookshelf

What is the uniform load on a 6″ wide by 36″ long grade M-2 particleboard shelf that is expected to support 60 pounds of books?

STEP 1: Calculate the area of the shelf (in square feet):

$$\text{Area of shelf} = \text{shelf width} \times \text{shelf length}$$

$$= 6'' \times 36''$$

$$= 216 \text{ square inches}$$

Convert square inches to square feet (see conversion table in appendix)

$$\text{Area of shelf} = 216 \text{ square inches} \times .00694 = 1.5 \text{ square feet}$$

STEP 2: Calculate the uniform load

$$\text{Uniform load} = \frac{\text{expected load on the shelf (in pounds)}}{\text{area of shelf (in square feet)}}$$

$$= \frac{60 \text{ pounds}}{1.5 \text{ square feet}}$$

$$= 40 \text{ pounds per square foot (psf)}$$

Once the uniform load is known, use it in conjunction with the chart to determine the thickness and maximum shelf length that can be used. As shown, for a uniform load of 40 psf, you have several shelf options: $\frac{1}{2}''$ thick by no more than 16″ long, $\frac{5}{8}''$ thick by no more than 20″ long, $\frac{3}{4}''$ thick by no more than 24″ long, 1″ thick by no more than 32″ long and $1\frac{1}{8}''$ thick by no more than 36″ long.

Since the shelf in our example is 36″ long, the grade M = 2 particleboard shelf must be at least $1\frac{1}{8}''$ thick.

CONCENTRATED LOADS

For a concentrated load, add a safety factor by dividing the expected load on the shelf by .625, then use the uniform load formula.

WOODSHOP APPLICATION
Calculating Concentrated Load on a Particleboard Shelf

You want to place a 60-pound workshop dehumidifier by itself in the center of a $\frac{3}{4}''$ thick by 10" wide by 36" long grade M-2 particleboard shelf. Can the shelf support the concentrated load?

STEP 1: Calculate concentrated load safety factor:

$$\text{Concentrated load safety factor} = \frac{\text{expected load on shelf (in pounds)}}{.625}$$

$$= \frac{60 \text{ pounds}}{.625}$$

$$= 96 \text{ pounds}$$

STEP 2: Calculate the area of the shelf (in square feet):

$$\text{Area of shelf} = \text{shelf width} \times \text{shelf length}$$

$$= 10'' \times 36''$$

$$= 360 \text{ square inches}$$

Convert square inches to square feet (see conversion table in appendix):

$$\text{Area of shelf} = 360 \text{ square inches} \times .00694 = 2.5 \text{ square feet}$$

STEP 3: Calculate the uniform load:

$$\text{Uniform load} = \frac{\text{expected load on the shelf (in pounds)}}{\text{area of shelf (in square feet)}}$$

$$= \frac{96 \text{ pounds}}{2.5 \text{ square feet}}$$

$$= 38.4 \text{ psf}$$

As shown in the chart, a $\frac{3}{4}''$-thick by 36" long shelf can only support a uniform load of 10 pounds. However, $1\frac{1}{8}''$-thick particleboard can support 45 pounds per square foot. Replace the $\frac{3}{4}''$-particleboard with $1\frac{1}{8}''$-thick particleboard.

MAXIMUM LOADS FOR PARTICLEBOARD SHELVING (FOR UNIFORMLY LOADED GRADE M-2 PARTICLEBOARD)

Shelf Span (inches)	Maximum Deflection (inches)	Uniform Load (pounds per square foot) Shelf Thickness (inches)				
		$\frac{1}{2}$	$\frac{5}{8}$	$\frac{3}{4}$	1	$1\frac{1}{8}$
16	.089	45	95	124	166	186
20	.111	20	45	80	130	146
24	.133	13	25	45	107	120
28	.156	8	15	25	70	100
32	.178	--	10	18	45	65
36	.200	--	5	10	30	45
40	.222	--	--	8	20	30
44	.244	--	--	5	15	25
48	.267	--	--	--	10	15
52	.289	--	--	--	8	10
56	.311	--	--	--	5	8
60	.333	--	--	--	--	5

Chart courtesy of the National Particleboard Association

DETERMINING BAND SAW BLADE LENGTH

Suppose it's time to replace your band saw blade, but you can't remember the blade length, and to make matters worse, you can't find the owner's manual. No need to despair, though, as this formula provides you with the correct length in short order.

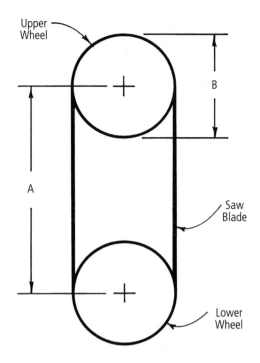

$L = (2 \times A) + (3.14 \times B)$

where:

L = band saw blade length (in inches)

A = distance between the band saw wheel center lines (in inches)

B = diameter of either the upper or lower wheel (in inches)

Note: Formula applies only to band saws that operate using a pair of same-sized wheels. Also, before measuring the A dimension, locate the adjustable upper (tension) wheel so it is midway between the fully up and fully down positions.

WOODSHOP APPLICATION
Determining the Length of a Band Saw Blade

You've purchased a used band saw at a garage sale, but the blade and owner's manual are missing. What's the correct blade length to buy?

STEP 1: Measure the distance between the band saw wheel center lines (in inches). Let's say it measures 20", therefore A = 20.

STEP 2: Measure the diameter of either the upper or lower wheel (in inches). Let's say it measures $12\frac{3}{4}''$, therefore B = $12\frac{3}{4}$ = 12.75.

STEP 3: Apply the formula.

$$L = (2 \times A) + (3.14 \times B)$$

$$L = (2 \times 20) + (3.14 \times 12.75)$$

$$L = 40 + 40.035$$

$$L = 80.035''$$

You'll want to buy the nearest standard blade length—in this case, 80".

PULLEY FORMULAS

Table saws, band saws, jointers, drill presses and lathes often incorporate a pair of pulleys and a V-belt to transfer power from the motor to the business end of the machine. When two pulleys operate from a common V-belt, they relate to each other according to the following formula:

A × B = C × D

A = speed (in rpms) of the motor

B = diameter (in inches) of the driver (motor) pulley

C = speed (in rpms) of the driven pulley

D = diameter (in inches) of the driven pulley

Note: The motor speed (in rpms) is usually stamped on the motor nameplate.

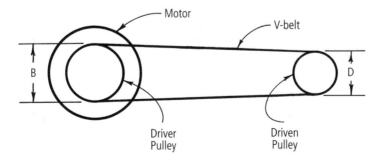

The previous formula can be rewritten, producing four additional formulas as follows:

$$A = \frac{C \times D}{B}$$

$$B = \frac{C \times D}{A}$$

$$C = \frac{A \times B}{D}$$

$$D = \frac{A \times B}{C}$$

WOODSHOP APPLICATION
Using the Pulley Formula

The motor on a lathe operates at 1725 rpm and has a 4″-diameter pulley. The motor pulley is connected by V-belt to a 2″ pulley that turns the lathe headstock. What is the lathe speed?

Based on the information given, the following is known:

A = 1725 rpm

B = 4″

C = driven pulley speed = lathe speed

D = 2″

Since C is unknown, use the formula:

$$C = \frac{A \times B}{D}$$

$$= \frac{1725 \times 4}{2}$$

$$= \frac{6900}{2}$$

$$= 3450 \text{ rpm}$$

TEMPERATURE CONVERSION FORMULAS

Use these formulas to convert from Celsius to Fahrenheit and vice versa.

To convert from Celsius to Fahrenheit use the formula:

$$F = (1.8 \times C) + 32$$

F = degrees Fahrenheit

C = degrees Celsius

To convert from Fahrenheit to Celsius use the formula:

$$C = .556 \times (F - 32)$$

C = degrees Celsius

F = degrees Fahrenheit

WOODSHOP APPLICATION

Using the Temperature Conversion Formulas

Convert 30° Celsius to degrees Fahrenheit.

$$F = (1.8 \times C) + 32$$

$$F = (1.8 \times 30) + 32$$

$$F = 54 + 32$$

$$F = 86°$$

Convert 68° Fahrenheit to Celsius.

$$C = .556 \times (F - 32)$$

$$C = .556 \times (68 - 32)$$

$$C = .556 \times 36$$

$$C = 20°$$

HOW TO CALCULATE BOARD FEET

The board foot (bf) is a measure of volume. One board foot is equal to 144 square inches or a board that measures 1″ thick (nominal dimension) by 12″ wide (nominal dimension) by 1′ long (actual dimension). The nominal dimension represents the thickness and width dimensions of a piece of lumber immediately after it is cut from a log.

3"
—
4
(1" Nominal)

$11\frac{1}{4}$"
(12" Nominal)

1'

Several formulas can be used to calculate board feet, but the one most often used is as follows:

$$\text{board feet} = \frac{\text{thickness (inches)} \times \text{width (inches)} \times \text{length (feet)}}{12}$$

To use the formula for any piece of lumber, multiply the thickness (in inches) by the width (in inches) by the length (in feet) and divide the resulting number by 12. Nominal dimensions *must* be used for the thickness and width.

WOODSHOP APPLICATION
Calculating Board Feet

How many board feet are in a 10′ length of 1×6 lumber.

STEP 1: Plug the numbers into the formula.

$$\text{Board feet} = \frac{1 \times 6 \times 10}{12}$$

STEP 2: Multiply the thickness, width and length.

$$\text{Board feet} = \frac{60}{12}$$

STEP 3: Divide the product by 12.

$$\text{Board feet} = 5$$

If you prefer to avoid math, the board footage chart that follows lists board footages for a variety of board sizes and lengths.

BOARD FOOTAGE CHART

Use this chart to determine board footages for the most common nominal sizes and lumber lengths. The chart also includes a column that shows the number of board feet per linear foot for each nominal size. For sizes not shown, see "How to Calculate Board Feet."

Nominal Size of Board (inches)	Board Feet per Linear Foot	Board Feet (to nearest 100th) Length of Board (feet)					
		6	8	10	12	14	16
$\frac{1}{2} \times 2$	0.0833	0.50	0.67	0.83	1.00	1.17	1.33
$\frac{1}{2} \times 3$	0.1250	0.75	1.00	1.25	1.50	1.75	2.00
$\frac{1}{2} \times 4$	0.1667	1.00	1.33	1.67	2.00	2.33	2.67
$\frac{1}{2} \times 6$	0.2500	1.50	2.00	2.50	3.00	3.50	4.00
$\frac{1}{2} \times 8$	0.3333	2.00	2.67	3.33	4.00	4.67	5.33
$\frac{1}{2} \times 10$	0.4167	2.50	3.33	4.17	5.00	5.83	6.67
$\frac{1}{2} \times 12$	0.5000	3.00	4.00	5.00	6.00	7.00	8.00
1×2	0.1667	1.00	1.33	1.67	2.00	2.33	2.67
1×3	0.2500	1.50	2.00	2.50	3.00	3.50	4.00
1×4	0.3333	2.00	2.67	3.33	4.00	4.67	5.33
1×6	0.5000	3.00	4.00	5.00	6.00	7.00	8.00
1×8	0.6667	4.00	5.33	6.67	8.00	9.33	10.67
1×10	0.8333	5.00	6.67	8.33	10.00	11.67	13.33
1×12	1.0000	6.00	8.00	10.00	12.00	14.00	16.00
2×2	0.3333	2.00	2.67	3.33	4.00	4.67	5.33
2×3	0.5000	3.00	4.00	5.00	6.00	7.00	8.00
2×4	0.6667	4.00	5.33	6.67	8.00	9.33	10.67
2×6	1.0000	6.00	8.00	10.00	12.00	14.00	16.00
2×8	1.3333	8.00	10.67	13.33	16.00	18.67	21.33
2×10	1.6667	10.00	13.33	16.67	20.00	23.33	26.67
2×12	2.0000	12.00	16.00	20.00	24.00	28.00	32.00
2×14	2.3333	14.00	18.67	23.33	28.00	32.67	37.33
3×3	0.7500	4.50	6.00	7.50	9.00	10.50	12.00
3×4	1.0000	6.00	8.00	10.00	12.00	14.00	16.00
3×6	1.5000	9.00	12.00	15.00	18.00	21.00	24.00
3×8	2.0000	12.00	16.00	20.00	24.00	28.00	32.00
3×10	2.5000	15.00	20.00	25.00	30.00	35.00	40.00
3×12	3.0000	18.00	24.00	30.00	36.00	42.00	48.00
3×14	3.5000	21.00	28.00	35.00	42.00	49.00	56.00
3×16	4.0000	24.00	32.00	40.00	48.00	56.00	64.00
4×4	1.3333	8.00	10.67	13.33	16.00	18.67	21.33
4×6	2.0000	12.00	16.00	20.00	24.00	28.00	32.00
4×8	2.6667	16.00	21.33	26.67	32.00	37.33	42.67
4×10	3.3333	20.00	26.67	33.33	40.00	46.67	53.33
4×12	4.0000	24.00	32.00	40.00	48.00	56.00	64.00
6×6	3.0000	18.00	24.00	30.00	36.00	42.00	48.00
6×8	4.0000	24.00	32.00	40.00	48.00	56.00	64.00
6×10	5.0000	30.00	40.00	50.00	60.00	70.00	80.00
6×12	6.0000	36.00	48.00	60.00	72.00	84.00	96.00

CALCULATING THE WEIGHT
OF A BOARD FOOT

It's often useful to know the weight of a project. For example, if you know the weight of a wall cabinet, you'll be better able to select a hanging system that provides adequate support for both the cabinet and its expected contents. If you plan to ship a project, commercial shippers want to know the project's weight. It's always a good idea to know the weight of a large project, like a chest of drawers, before you start muscling it around the woodshop. Indeed, if the calculations show the chest is going to be a backbreaker, you can enlist helpers before starting to move the piece around.

In most books and technical tables, the weights of various wood species are shown in terms of either the **density** or the **specific gravity**. An abbreviated specific gravity table, listing some commonly used woods, is included here. You'll find more extensive tables in books on the subject of wood identification. Check your library.

Density is a measure of a material's weight per unit volume, usually shown as weight per cubic foot or, in the metric system, as kilograms per cubic meter. Unlike many other materials, wood is hygroscopic, which means it takes on or gives off water based the relative humidity of the surrounding air. Wood densities, therefore, are a measure of the weight of the wood material *and* the water in the wood. Since the weight of wood can change when the relative humidity changes, most tables specify the densities at a particular moisture content.

The specific gravity provides another way to look at density. As a general definition, the specific gravity of any solid or liquid is the ratio of the density of the material to the density of water. In most technical tables, when considering wood, the cubic foot is used as the measure of volume, therefore the specific gravity is often defined as the ratio of a cubic foot of wood to a cubic foot of water. To account for the hygroscopic characteristics of wood, most technical tables indicate specific gravity based on weight when oven-dry and volume when at 12 percent moisture content.

Keep in mind that the specific gravity is based on average species characteristics, which means that the number could vary a bit from board to board.

SOME USEFUL FORMULAS RELATED TO DENSITY, SPECIFIC GRAVITY AND THE WEIGHT OF WOOD

To calculate the density when you know the specific gravity, use this formula:

$$D = S \times 62.4$$

D = the density of wood (in pounds per cubic foot)

S = the average specific gravity of oven-dry wood

Example:

Eastern white pine has an average specific gravity of .35 (at oven-dry weight and volume at 12 percent moisture content). What is the density?

$$D = .35 \times 62.4$$

$$D = 21.84 \text{ pounds per cubic foot}$$

To calculate the average specific gravity when you know the density, use this formula:

$$S = \frac{D}{62.4}$$

S = the average specific gravity of oven-dry wood

D = the density of wood (in pounds per cubic foot)

Example:

The density of black cherry (at oven-dry weight and volume at 12 percent moisture content) is 31.2 pounds per cubic foot. What is the average specific gravity?

$$S = \frac{31.2}{62.4}$$

$$S = .5$$

To calculate the weight of a board foot (in pounds) when you know the density, use this formula:

$$W = \frac{D}{12}$$

W = weight of a board foot (in pounds)

D = density of the wood (in pounds per cubic foot)

Example:

White oak has a density of 42.4 pounds per cubic foot (at oven-dry weight and volume at 12 percent moisture content). What is the weight of one board foot?

$$W = \frac{42.4}{12}$$

$$W = 3.53 \text{ pounds per board foot}$$

To calculate the weight of a board foot (in pounds) when you know the average specific gravity, use this formula:

$$W = \frac{S \times 62.4}{12}$$

W = weight of a board foot (in pounds)

S = average specific gravity of the wood species when oven-dry

Example:

The average specific gravity of black walnut is .55 (at oven-dry weight and volume at 12 percent moisture content). What is the weight of one board foot?

$$W = \frac{.55 \times 62.4}{12}$$

$$W = \frac{34.32}{12}$$

$$W = 2.86 \text{ pounds per board foot}$$

Table of Specific Gravity

Common Name	Botanical Name	Average Specific Gravity*
Ash, White	Fraxinus americana	.60
Basswood	Tilia americana	.37
Beech	Fagus grandifolia	.64
Birch, Yellow	Betula alleghaniensis	.62
Butternut	Juglans cinerea	.38
Cedar, Eastern Red	Juniperus virginiana	.47
Cherry, Black	Prunus serotina	.50
Chestnut, American	Castenea dentata	.43
Douglas Fir	Pseudotsuga menziesii	.48
Ebony	Diospyros spp.	.90
Lignum Vitae	Guaiacum spp.	1.14
Mahogany, African	Khaya spp.	.63
Maple, Red	Acer rubrum	.54
Maple, Sugar	Acer saccharum	.63
Oak, Northern Red	Quercus rubra	.63
Oak, White	Quercus alba	.68
Pine, Idaho White	Pinus monticola	.38
Pine, Eastern White	Pinus strobus	.35
Pine, Longleaf	Pinus palustris	.58
Pine, Ponderosa	Pinus ponderosa	.40
Pine, Shortleaf	Pinus echinata	.51
Pine, Sugar	Pinus lambertiana	.36
Poplar, Yellow	Liriodendron tulipifera	.42
Redwood	Sequoia sempervirens	.40
Spruce, Sitka	Picea sitchensis	.40
Teak	Tectona grandis	.57
Walnut, Black	Juglans nigra	.55

* At oven-dry weight and volume at 12 percent moisture content

WOODSHOP APPLICATION
Determining the Weight of a Tabletop

A rectangular tabletop made from 1″ (nominal thickness) black cherry measures 3′ wide and 6′ long. What is the approximate weight of the tabletop?

STEP 1: Determine the number of board feet in the tabletop.

(Helpful hint: Consider the tabletop as one big board and apply the board footage formula to the entire tabletop.)

$$\text{board feet} = \frac{\text{thickness (inches)} \times \text{width (inches)} \times \text{length (feet)}}{12}$$

$$= \frac{1 \times 36 \times 6}{12}$$

$$= \frac{216}{12} = 18 \text{ board feet}$$

STEP 2: Use the table to find the average specific gravity of black cherry.

From the table, black cherry has an average specific gravity of 0.50.

STEP 3: Apply the formula to determine the weight per board foot.

$$W = \frac{5 \times 62.4}{12}$$

$$W = \frac{.50 \times 62.4}{12}$$

$$W = \frac{31.2}{12}$$

$$W = 2.60 \text{ pounds per board foot.}$$

STEP 4: Multiply the board footage of the tabletop by the weight per board foot.

$$18 \times 2.60 = 46.8 \text{ pounds}$$

The tabletop weighs 46.8 pounds based on an oven-dry (zero moisture content) weight. Since the actual moisture content of the tabletop is likely to be in the 6 to 12 percent range, you can expect the tabletop to weigh slightly more than the calculated amount.

CHAPTER 15

Converting a Photograph Into a Dimensioned Drawing

From time to time, most woodworkers will come across a book or magazine containing a photograph of a furniture piece that would be wonderful to build—if only there were some dimensions from which to work. You might be surprised to learn that with a little savvy and the help of some simple math almost any photograph can be coaxed into giving up some of those dimensions. The math used is based on the principles of **ratio** and **proportion**.

RATIO

A ratio compares two numbers by using division. Let's say you have a box containing 10 wood screws and 25 washers. The ratio of wood screws to washers is $\frac{10}{25}$. By dividing both the numerator and denominator by 5, the ratio can be reduced to $\frac{2}{5}$. Put another way, for every 2 wood screws there are 5 washers. The ratio can also be written as $2 \div 5$ or $2:5$. The symbol : is called the **ratio sign**.

In the same box, the ratio of washers to wood screws is $\frac{25}{10}$, which reduces to $\frac{5}{2}$. In other words, for every 5 washers there are 2 wood screws.

Let's consider another example. The top of a coffee table measures 18″ wide by 48″ long. The ratio of the width to the length is $\frac{18}{48}$, which reduces to $\frac{3}{8}$. For every 3″ of width, the tabletop has 8″ of length.

For the same tabletop, the ratio of the length to the width is $\frac{48}{18}$, or $\frac{8}{3}$. For every 8″ of length, there are 3″ of width.

PROPORTION

A proportion shows that two ratios are equal, for example, $\frac{1}{2} = \frac{5}{10}$, which can also be written as $1:2 :: 5:10$. The symbol :: is called the **proportion sign**. When a proportion is set up in this manner, the inside numbers (2 and 5) are called the **means**, while the outside numbers (1 and 10) are called the **extremes**. Examples of other proportions are $\frac{2}{3} = \frac{6}{9}$, $\frac{8}{5} = \frac{16}{10}$ and $\frac{1}{4} = \frac{4}{16}$.

THE CROSS PRODUCT RULE

The **cross product rule** states that, in any proportion, the product of the means equals the product of the extremes. Therefore:

$$a:b \,::\, c:d$$

$$\frac{a}{b} = \frac{c}{d}$$

$$ad = bc$$

The equation can also be written as:

$$a = \frac{bc}{d}$$

$$b = \frac{ad}{c}$$

$$c = \frac{ad}{b}$$

$$d = \frac{bc}{a}$$

Let's look at the proportion $1:2 \,::\, 5:10$ and see if it checks out.

$$1:2 \,::\, 5:10$$

$$\frac{1}{2} = \frac{5}{10}$$

$$1 \times 10 = 2 \times 5$$

$$10 = 10$$

Since $10 = 10$, the ratios $1:2$ and $5:10$ are in proportion.

USING PROPORTION TO DIMENSION A PHOTOGRAPH

Let's say you spot this handsome drop leaf table in a magazine. It's a piece you'd love to build if you had some dimensions. Here's how to get them using the principles of ratio and proportion.

STEP 1: Find something in the photo that can provide a clue to the scale.

This step takes some creative guesswork. Begin by looking for any item in the photo that has a generally standard size. It could be a coffee mug, a dinner dish or a hardcover book. The sizes of these items are somewhat standard: a 4″ height for a coffee mug, a 10″ diameter for a dinner plate and a 10″ to 12″ height for a hardcover book. The item could be a nearby piece of furniture that is built to standard dimensions. For example, the seat height for a chair is usually 17″ to $18\frac{1}{2}$″. Once you find a standard-sized item, assign it a dimension.

If you can't find standard-sized item in the photo, you'll need to assign a dimension to some part of the piece. For example, if the piece is a wall cabinet, decide how tall or wide you want it to be, then assign a dimension to either the height or width.

All subsequent dimensions will be based on your assigned dimension, so try to be as accurate as you can. If possible, work with vertical measurements, as diagonal and horizontal measurements sometimes appear shorter due to the camera angle.

The picture provides only one clue to the table's size. All tables typically measure 29″ to 31″ in height. Since 30″ is a good average, let's go with that. Already the photo has given up one dimension: The table's height is 30″.

STEP 2: Calculate the working ratio.

Measure the table height directly from the photograph. You should find it measures just about 2″. Since we know the actual table height is 30″, the ratio of the photo height to actual height is $\frac{2}{30}$, which reduces to $\frac{1}{15}$. This ratio, called the **working ratio**, is the one you will use to calculate all the remaining dimensions.

STEP 3: Calculate the tabletop length.

Next, measure the table length directly from the photograph. It should measure about 4″. The cross product rule can now be applied, since you know three of the four terms.

$$\frac{a}{b} = \frac{c}{d}$$

a = 1″

b = 15″

c = 4″

d = unknown

$$\frac{1}{15} = \frac{4}{d}$$

Using the cross product formula for d:

$$d = \frac{bc}{a}$$

$$d = \frac{15 \times 4}{1}$$

$$d = 60″$$

The tabletop is 60″ long.

STEP 4: Calculate the width of the drop leaves.

Measure the width of the front drop leaf directly from the photograph. It should measure about $\frac{5}{8}$″. Applying the cross product rule you have:

$$\frac{a}{b} = \frac{c}{d}$$

a = 1″

b = 15″

c = $\frac{5}{8}$″ = .625″

d = unknown

Using the cross product formula for d:

$$d = \frac{bc}{a}$$

$$d = \frac{15 \times .625}{1}$$

$$d = 9.375″ = 9\frac{3}{8}″$$

Each drop leaf is $9\frac{3}{8}$″ wide.

STEP 5: Determine the width of the tabletop.

Because of the camera angle, the tabletop width appears shortened in the photo. Since there is no way to measure the full width of the tabletop from the photo, you'll need to come up with a dimension on your own.

As a general rule, a drop leaf table like this will have a tabletop width that measures about twice the width of a leaf. Or, to put it another way, the ratio of tabletop width to leaf width is $\frac{2}{1}$. Since you know the actual width of the leaf, you can use the cross product formula to find the width of the tabletop.

Applying the cross product rule you have:

$$\frac{a}{b} = \frac{c}{d}$$

$a = 2$

$b = 1$

$c = $ unknown

$d = 9\frac{3}{8}'' = 9.375''$

Using the cross product formula for c:

$$c = \frac{ad}{b}$$

$$c = \frac{2 \times 9.375}{1}$$

$$c = 18.75'' = 18\frac{3}{4}''$$

The tabletop measures $18\frac{3}{4}''$ wide.

STEP 6: Calculate the upper width of the tapered leg.

The drop leaf covers the upper part of the tapered leg, so measure the leg width at the highest visible point. It should measure about $\frac{7}{64}''$ wide.

Applying the cross product rule you have:

$$\frac{a}{b} = \frac{c}{d}$$

$a = 1''$

$b = 15''$

$c = \frac{7}{64}'' = .109375''$

$d = $ unknown

Using the cross product formula for d:

$$d = \frac{bc}{a}$$

$$d = \frac{15 \times .109375}{1}$$

$$d = 1.641'', \text{ or just under } 1\frac{11}{16}''$$

Since the taper leg is going to be slightly wider above the point where it was measured on the photograph, it's a pretty safe assumption that the leg is made from $1\frac{3}{4}''$-wide stock. Also, since legs on similar tables are almost always made from square stock, it can be reasonably assumed that the legs are made from $1\frac{3}{4}''$-square stock.

STEP 7: Calculate the lower width of the tapered leg.

The lower end of the leg should measure about $\frac{1}{16}''$.

Applying the cross product rule you have:

$$\frac{a}{b} = \frac{c}{d}$$

$a = 1''$

$b = 15''$

$c = \frac{1}{16}'' = .0625''$

$d = $ unknown

Using the cross product formula for d:

$$d = \frac{bc}{a}$$

$$d = \frac{15 \times .0625}{1}$$

$$d = .9375'' \text{ (round to } 1'')$$

The leg tapers to $1''$ inch at the bottom. (Typically, tables like this have legs that are tapered on only the two inside faces, rather than on all four faces.)

STEP 8: Determine the width of the aprons.

The leaves prevent you from seeing the table frame, but drop leaf tables usually use four aprons to tie the legs together. For a table this size, $5''$-wide aprons should provide adequate strength.

STEP 9: Determine the apron joinery.

Dowels can be used to join the end of each apron to a leg, but a mortise-and-tenon joint is more traditional and will provide greater strength.

STEP 10: The drop leaf support system.

The drop leaf support system is completely hidden by the front leaf. To get that information, you'll need to review a good woodworking design book. Several simple systems are commonly used.

CHAPTER 16
Reading the Micrometer and Vernier Caliper

Carpenter's rules, tape measures and steel rules are the workhorses when it comes to measuring in the woodshop. Although most of these tools are, at best, accurate to $\frac{1}{64}''$, that's sufficient accuracy for most woodshop applications. Occasionally, however, it can be valuable to measure more accurately, and that's where a micrometer or vernier caliper can come in handy. Indeed, most micrometers and vernier calipers are accurate to $\frac{1}{1000}''$ (.001″).

Micrometers and vernier calipers can be put to good use measuring the thickness of veneer, sheet metal, plastic laminate (e.g., Formica), acrylic sheet (e.g., Plexiglas), thin plywood, and miscellaneous hardware, including hinges. In addition, the measuring tools can be used to accurately check the diameters of bolts, screws, nails, brads, machine threads and the like. Vernier calipers, which can also check inside diameters, are ideally suited for measuring drilled holes, the inside diameters of bushings and the widths of dadoes and grooves.

Manufactures of micrometers and vernier calipers also offer models with dial calipers and digital readouts. Both options make the tools easier to read. However, that convenience comes at a price, particularly if you want a digital version. The information in this chapter is based on using the basic models which do not incorporate a dial caliper or digital readout.

THE MICROMETER
The micrometer is a precision instrument for measuring thicknesses and diameters (Fig. 16-1). Indeed, you'll find that most models are accurate to $\frac{1}{1000}''$ (.001″), which is plenty accurate for woodshop applications. Metric models are also available, but our discussion will be limited to micrometers that measure in inches. Micrometers are sold in a

Fig. 16-1

Photo courtesy of the L.S. Starrett Company

variety of size ranges: 0″ to $\frac{1}{2}$″, 0″ to 1″, 1″ to 2″, 2″ to 3″, and so on, up to 23″ to 24″. In the woodshop, the micrometer is used mostly for taking small measurements, so the 0″ to 1″ size range generally proves to be the most practical size.

READING THE MICROMETER

With an array of moving parts and numbered lines, the micrometer might look a little imposing to the uninitiated. Actually, I think you'll find it's easy to read. Basically, you work with just two numbered lines: those on the sleeve and those on the thimble (Fig. 16-2).

Sleeve ——— Thimble

Fig. 16-2   Illustration courtesy of the L.S. Starrett Company

Lines on the Sleeve

As shown in Fig. 16-2, the reading line on the sleeve is divided into 40 parts, each part representing .025″. Micrometers are designed so one full revolution of the thimble moves the spindle face .025″. Every fourth line is extended and represents 4 × .025 or $\frac{100}{1000}$″ (.100″).

The extended lines on the sleeve are marked 0, 1, 2, 3, 4 and so on through 10. The line marked 1 represents $\frac{100}{1000}$″ (.100″), the line marked 2 represents $\frac{200}{1000}$″ (.200″), the line marked 3 represents $\frac{300}{1000}$″ (.300″), and so on, through 10, which represents $\frac{1000}{1000}$″ or 1″.

Lines on the Thimble

As shown in Fig. 16-2, the circumference of the thimble is divided into 25 equal parts, numbered from 0 to 25, with each part representing $\frac{1}{1000}$″ (.001″). The line marked 1 represents $\frac{1}{1000}$″ (.001″), the line marked 2 represents $\frac{2}{1000}$″ (.002″), and so on, through 25, which completes a revolution of the thimble and represents $\frac{25}{1000}$″ (.025″).

TAKING A MEASUREMENT

When measuring most small parts, the micrometer is held as shown in Fig. 16-3. Place the part against the micrometer anvil with the left hand, then use the thumb and index finger of your right hand to turn the thimble. Turn the thimble until the face of the spindle *lightly* contacts the part. Take the reading while the part remains in the micrometer. If it's difficult to take a reading with the part in the micrometer, lock the spindle at the final setting, then remove the part and take the reading.

Fig. 16-3   Photo courtesy of the L.S. Starrett Company

Here's how to read a micrometer.

STEP 1: Read the sleeve. To do this, multiply the number of vertical divisions *visible* on the sleeve by .025".

STEP 2: Read the thimble by determining the thimble number that aligns with the reading line on the sleeve. Multiply the number by .001.

STEP 3: Add the product from step 1 to the product from step 2.
Let's look at an example.

Example: Read the micrometer setting shown in Fig. 16-2.

STEP 1: Read the sleeve. Seven vertical divisions are visible, so 7 × .025 = .175".

STEP 2: Read the thimble. The number three aligns with the reading line on the sleeve. Each number represents .001, therefore 3 × .001 = .003"

STEP 3: Add the product from step 1 to the product in step 2.

$$
\begin{array}{r}
.175 \\
+ .003 \\
\hline
.178
\end{array}
$$

The micrometer reads .178".

THE VERNIER CALIPER

Like the micrometer, the vernier caliper (Fig. 16-4) is a precision instrument for measuring thicknesses and diameters. Unlike the micrometer, it can also measure inside diameters. Most models are accurate to $\frac{1}{1000}$" (.001"). Metric models are also available, as are models that can be read both in inches and millimeters.

Fig. 16-4   Photo courtesy of the L.S. Starrett Company

Vernier calipers are sold in several size ranges: 0" to 6", 0" to 12", 0" to 24", and so on, up to a whopping 0" to 72". Since a woodshop vernier caliper is used mostly for taking small measurements, the 0" to 6" size range is suitable for most applications.

READING THE VERNIER CALIPER

The vernier caliper, like the micrometer, might appear to be a challenging tool to master. It's not. You use just two number lines: those on the stationary bar and on the vernier slide assemble. However, if you are at all like me and your eyesight isn't as strong as it once was, a good pair of reading glasses is a must when using this tool.

Keep in mind that some models might have different divisions on the stationary bar and vernier slide assembly, but the basic reading procedure remains the same. Refer to the manufacturer's instructions included with your tool.

Lines on the Stationary Bar

On the model shown (Fig. 16-5), the top and bottom edges on the stationary bar are measured in inches. Each inch is divided into 20 parts, with each part marked by a line that represents $\frac{50}{1000}$" (.050"). Note that every second line is extended a bit and numbered 1 through 10; therefore each numbered line represents $\frac{100}{1000}$" (.100"). The lines on the lower edge of the bar are used to make outside measurements, while the lines on the upper edge of the bar are used to make inside measurements.

Lines on the Vernier Plate

The vernier plate (Fig. 16-5) is divided into 50 parts, each part marked by a line that represents $\frac{1}{1000}$" (.001"). Every fifth line is numbered, so the numbers read 5, 10, 15, 20, and so on, up to 50. Note on this model the top plate is used for making inside measurements, while the bottom plate is used for making outside measurements.

50 Divisions
Vernier Plate
Stationary Bar

Fig. 16-5   Photo courtesy of the L.S. Starrett Company

TAKING A MEASUREMENT

To measure *outside* dimensions of most small parts, place the part against the inside face of the caliper's fixed jaw, then slide the vernier assembly until the inside face of the movable jaw *lightly* contacts the part. To measure *inside* dimensions of most small parts, place both the fixed and movable nibs inside the part to be measured, then slide the vernier assembly until the outside faces of the nibs *lightly* contact the part.

Here's how to read a vernier caliper.

STEP 1: Read the number of full inches on the stationary bar up to the zero point on the vernier plate. Use the lower plate if taking outside measurements; use the upper plate if taking inside measurements.

STEP 2: Read the number of lines from the last full inch mark to the zero point on the vernier plate. Multiply the number of lines by .050 inch.

STEP 3: Starting from the zero point on the vernier plate, scan across the plate until you find a line on the vernier plate that aligns with a line on the stationary bar. (This is where reading glasses are a must for me.) Count the number of lines on the vernier plate from the zero point to the two lines that aligned. Multiply the number of lines by .001″.

STEP 4: Add the numbers from steps 1, 2 and 3.

Let's look at a couple examples.

Example 1: Read the vernier caliper setting shown in Fig. 16-5. Assume it is an *outside* measurement.

STEP 1: Read the number of full inches on the stationary bar up to the zero point on the *lower* vernier plate. Note that 3 full inches are shown.

STEP 2: Read the number of lines from the last full inch mark to the zero point on the lower vernier plate. Multiply the number of lines by .050″. There are 14 lines from the 3″ line to the zero point on the lower vernier plate; 14 × .050 = .700″.

STEP 3: Starting from the zero point on the lower vernier plate, scan across the plate until you find a line on the plate that aligns with a line on the stationary bar. Count the number of lines on the lower vernier plate from the zero point to the two lines that aligned. On the lower plate, the third line from the zero point aligns with a line on the stationary bar; $3 \times .001 = .003''$.

STEP 4: Add the numbers from steps 1, 2 and 3.

$$
\begin{array}{r}
3.000 \\
.700 \\
+ \ .003 \\
\hline
3.703
\end{array}
$$

The vernier caliper reads 3.703″.

Example 2: Read the vernier caliper setting shown in Fig. 16-5. Assume it is an *inside* measurement.

STEP 1: Read the number of full inches on the stationary bar up to the zero point on the *upper* vernier plate. Note that 4 full inches are shown.

STEP 2: Read the number of lines from the last full inch mark to the zero point on the upper vernier plate. Multiply the number of lines by .050 inch. In this example, there are no lines.

STEP 3: Starting from the zero point on the upper vernier plate, scan across the plate until you find a line on the plate that aligns with a line on the stationary bar. Count the number of lines on the upper vernier plate from the zero point to the two lines that aligned. On the upper plate, the second line from the zero point aligns with a line on the stationary bar; $2 \times .001 = .002''$.

STEP 4: Add the numbers from steps 1, 2 and 3.

$$
\begin{array}{r}
4.000 \\
.000 \\
+ \ .002 \\
\hline
4.002
\end{array}
$$

The vernier caliper reads 4.002″.

APPENDIX

Glossary

Acute Angle An angle less than 90°.

Angle The space between two straight lines that meet.

Angle Sides The straight lines that meet to form an angle.

Arc A portion of the circumference.

Area A measure of the amount of surface on a figure. See *surface area.*

Base 1. A factor that is repeatedly multiplied. 2. The end of a prism.

Bisect To divide in half.

Canceling A means of reducing a fraction by dividing the numerator and denominator by a common factor.

Chord A straight line connecting two points on a circle.

Circle A closed curve, with all points equally distant from the center.

Circumference The distance around a circle.

Common Denominator A denominator that two or more fractions share.

Common Multiplier or Common Number A number that, when multiplied by the numerator and denominator of a fraction, raises the fraction to a higher term.

Compound Angle Cut The angle created when a workpiece is cut at an angle other than 90° using a saw blade that is also at an angle other than 90°.

Concentric Circles Two or more circles with the same center point but different diameters.

Cone A solid with a circular base whose lateral surface narrows to a point at the top.

Cube A regular solid with six square face surfaces. See *Hexahedron.*

Cube Root A factor multiplied three times to produce a power.

Cylinder A solid bounded by two equal, parallel circles and by a curve surface formed by moving a straight line of fixed length so the ends lie on the two parallel circles.

Decimal A means of expressing a fraction that has a denominator of ten or some multiple of ten.

Decimal Point A period mark used to separate a whole number from a decimal.

Denominator The bottom part of a fraction.

Density A measure of a material's weight per unit volume.

Diameter A straight line that passes through the center of a circle and extends from one side of the circle to the other.

Digit One of the ten symbols 0 through 9.

Dividend The number to be divided by another number.

Divisor The number divided into another number.

Eccentric Circles Two or more circles with different center points.

Ellipse An oval-shaped closed curve.

Equation A statement showing that two numbers or two groups of numbers are equal.

Equilateral Triangle A triangle with sides of equal length.

Equivalent Fraction A fraction with the same value as another fraction.

Expanded Form A number broken down into its component groups of ten or multiples of ten.

Exponent A small, raised number written adjacent to a base number indicating the number of times the base number must be repeatedly multiplied.

Factor A number that, when multiplied by another number, results in a product.

Formula An equation that shows a unique relationship between certain things.

Fraction One or more of the equal parts of a whole.

Fraction Bar or Fraction Line The short, straight line drawn between the numerator and denominator of a fraction.

Grid Square Method (for enlarging patterns) A method for enlarging grid patterns using a grid of squares.

Hexahedron A regular solid with six square face surfaces. See *Cube.*

Horizontal Line A straight line parallel to the horizon.

Hypotenuse In a right triangle, the side opposite the right angle.

Improper fraction A fraction with a numerator that is equal to or greater than the denominator.

Index A small, raised number written to the left of the radical sign indicating how many times the equal factors are multiplied to produce the number within the radical sign.

Irregular Curved Line A curved line with a radius that constantly changes.

Isosceles Triangle A triangle with two sides of equal length.

Lateral Face The side of a prism.

LCD The smallest number that is evenly divisible by the denominators of a group of fractions. See *Lowest Common Denominator*.

Like Fractions Fractions with the same denominator.

Line A straight line.

Lowest Common Denominator The smallest number that is evenly divisible by the denominators of a group of fractions. See *LCD*.

Mixed Number A number made up of a whole number and a fraction.

Numerator The top part of a fraction.

Oblique Cone A cone whose axis is not perpendicular to the base.

Oblique Cylinder A cylinder whose lateral surface is not perpendicular to the base.

Oblique Line A straight line that is neither horizontal nor vertical.

Oblique Rectangular Prism A prism with lateral faces not perpendicular to a rectangular base.

Oblique Square Pyramid A pyramid with the axis not perpendicular to a square base.

Obtuse Angle An angle that is more than 90° but less than 180°.

Obtuse Triangle A triangle with an obtuse angle.

Parallel Lines Two or more straight lines that remain the same distance apart at all points.

Perimeter The distance around any closed plane figure.

Perpendicular Lines Straight lines that intersect at 90°.

Photocopy Method (for enlarging patterns) A method for enlarging grid patterns using a photocopier.

Place Value The location of a digit in a number.

Plane Figure A shape that has length and width, but no depth.

Plus Sign The symbol (+) used to indicate a positive number or the operation of addition.

Polygon A closed plane figure that has three or more sides and three or more angles.

Power The product of a factor that is repeatedly multiplied.

Prism A solid with two parallel bases that are identical polygons.

Proper Fraction A fraction with a numerator that is less than the denominator.

Proportion A statement that shows two ratios are equal.

Proportion Sign The symbol (::) used to indicate proportion.

Pyramid A solid with a polygon for its base and triangles for its sides.

Quadrilateral A polygon with four sides and four angles.

Quotient The number that results from the division of two numbers.

Radical Sign The symbol ($\sqrt{}$) used to indicate the root of number.

Radius A straight line extending from the center of a circle to any point on the circle.

Ratio A comparison of two numbers using division.

Rectangle A four-sided figure with four right angles.

Reduced Fraction A fraction written in its lowest terms. See *Simplest Form*.

Regular Decagon A figure having ten equal-length sides and ten equal angles.

Regular Dodecagon A figure having twelve equal-length sides and twelve equal angles.

Regular Hexagon A figure having six equal-length sides and six equal angles.

Regular Octagon A figure having eight equal-length sides and eight equal angles.

Regular Pentagon A figure having five equal-length sides and five equal angles.

Regular Polygon A polygon with all angles equal and all sides of equal length.

Regular Solid A solid with face surfaces that are regular polygons.

Rhomboid A four-sided figure with opposite sides parallel, adjacent sides unequal, and usually having two acute angles and two obtuse angles.

Rhombus A four-sided figure with all sides of equal length, opposite sides parallel, and usually having two acute angles and two obtuse angles.

Right Angle The angle formed by the intersection of a straight line perpendicular to another straight line and measuring 90°.

Right Cone A cone with the axis perpendicular to the base.

Right Cylinder A cylinder whose lateral surface is perpendicular to the base.

Right Rectangular Prism A prism with a lateral face perpendicular to a rectangular base.

Right Square Prism A prism with a lateral face perpendicular to a square base.

Right Square Pyramid A pyramid with the axis perpendicular to a square base.

Right Triangle A triangle with one 90° angle.

Right Triangular Pyramid A pyramid with the axis perpendicular to a triangular base.

Root (of a number) A factor that when repeatedly multiplied produces the number.

Scalene Triangle A triangle with all sides unequal in length.

Segment The part of a circle cut off by a straight line.

Semicircle One-half of a circle.

Simplest Form A fraction written in its lowest terms. See *Reduced Fraction*.

Simplifying The process of reducing a fraction to its lowest terms.

Solid Figure A shape that has length, width and depth.

Specific Gravity (of a solid or liquid) A ratio of the density of a material to the density of water.

Sphere A round, solid figure in which every point on the surface is the same distance from the center.

Square A four-sided figure with four right angles and four equal-length sides.

Square Root A factor of a number that when multiplied by itself gives the number.

Straight Angle An angle formed by two lines that intersect to form a straight line and measuring 180°.

Straight Line The shortest distance between two points.

Surface Area A measure of the amount of surface on a figure. See *Area*.

Tangent A straight line that touches a circle at only one point.

Terms The numerator and denominator of a fraction.

Tetrahedron A regular solid with four triangular face surfaces.

Theorem In geometry, any statement or rule that can be proved to be true.

Trapezium A four-sided figure having no sides parallel.

Trapezoid A four-sided figure with two sides parallel and two sides not parallel.

Triangle A polygon with three sides and three angles.

Triangular Prism A prism with a triangular base.

Trisect To divide into thirds.

Truncated Pyramid The portion that remains after a cutting plane is passed through a pyramid.

Truncated Right Cone The portion that remains after a cutting plane is passed through a right cone.

Unlike Fractions Fractions with different denominators.

Vertex The point where two angle sides meet to form an angle.

Vertical Line A straight line perpendicular to the horizon.

Volume A measure of the three-dimensional size of a solid figure.

Whole Number Any number that is not a fraction or a decimal.

Conversion Charts

Fractions to Decimal Equivalents

Fraction (in lowest terms) (inches)	Decimal Equivalents (inches)	Fraction (in lowest terms) (inches)	Decimal Equivalents (inches)
$\frac{1}{64}$	.015625	$\frac{33}{64}$	.515625
$\frac{1}{32}$	.031250	$\frac{17}{32}$	.531250
$\frac{3}{64}$	.046875	$\frac{35}{64}$	.546875
$\frac{1}{16}$	.062500	$\frac{9}{16}$	.562500
$\frac{5}{64}$	.078125	$\frac{37}{64}$	.578125
$\frac{3}{32}$	.093750	$\frac{19}{32}$	.593750
$\frac{7}{64}$	.109375	$\frac{39}{64}$	.609375
$\frac{1}{8}$	.125000	$\frac{5}{8}$	.625000
$\frac{9}{64}$	.140625	$\frac{41}{64}$	.640625
$\frac{5}{32}$	.156250	$\frac{21}{32}$	.656250
$\frac{11}{64}$	.171875	$\frac{43}{64}$	.671875
$\frac{3}{16}$	.187500	$\frac{11}{16}$	.687500
$\frac{13}{64}$	.203125	$\frac{45}{64}$	.703125
$\frac{7}{32}$	.218750	$\frac{23}{32}$	.718750
$\frac{15}{64}$	.234375	$\frac{47}{64}$	.734375
$\frac{1}{4}$	.250000	$\frac{3}{4}$	.750000
$\frac{17}{64}$	.265625	$\frac{49}{64}$	.765625
$\frac{9}{32}$	.281250	$\frac{25}{32}$	.781250
$\frac{19}{64}$	.296875	$\frac{51}{64}$	.796875
$\frac{5}{16}$	.312500	$\frac{13}{16}$	.812500
$\frac{21}{64}$	.328125	$\frac{53}{64}$	.828125
$\frac{11}{32}$	.343750	$\frac{27}{32}$	.843750
$\frac{23}{64}$	.359375	$\frac{55}{64}$	.859375
$\frac{3}{8}$	.375000	$\frac{7}{8}$	.875000
$\frac{25}{64}$	.390625	$\frac{57}{64}$	.890625
$\frac{13}{32}$	.406250	$\frac{29}{32}$	.906250
$\frac{27}{64}$	.421875	$\frac{59}{64}$	.921875
$\frac{7}{16}$	.437500	$\frac{15}{16}$	.937500
$\frac{29}{64}$	.453125	$\frac{61}{64}$	.953125
$\frac{15}{32}$	.468750	$\frac{31}{32}$	.968750
$\frac{31}{64}$	.484375	$\frac{63}{64}$	.984375
$\frac{1}{2}$	.500000	$\frac{1}{1}$	1.00000

Fractions to Metric Equivalents

Fraction (in lowest terms) (inches)	Metric Equivalents (millimeters)	Fraction (in lowest terms) (inches)	Metric Equivalents (millimeters)
$\frac{1}{64}$	0.396875	$\frac{33}{64}$	13.096880
$\frac{1}{32}$	0.793750	$\frac{17}{32}$	13.493750
$\frac{3}{64}$	1.190625	$\frac{35}{64}$	13.890630
$\frac{1}{16}$	1.587500	$\frac{9}{16}$	14.287500
$\frac{5}{64}$	1.984375	$\frac{37}{64}$	14.684380
$\frac{3}{32}$	2.381250	$\frac{19}{32}$	15.081250
$\frac{7}{64}$	2.778125	$\frac{39}{64}$	15.478130
$\frac{1}{8}$	3.175000	$\frac{5}{8}$	15.875000
$\frac{9}{64}$	3.571875	$\frac{41}{64}$	16.271880
$\frac{5}{32}$	3.968750	$\frac{21}{32}$	16.668750
$\frac{11}{64}$	4.365625	$\frac{43}{64}$	17.065630
$\frac{3}{16}$	4.762500	$\frac{11}{16}$	17.462500
$\frac{13}{64}$	5.159375	$\frac{45}{64}$	17.859380
$\frac{7}{32}$	5.556250	$\frac{23}{32}$	18.256250
$\frac{15}{64}$	5.953125	$\frac{47}{64}$	18.653130
$\frac{1}{4}$	6.350000	$\frac{3}{4}$	19.050000
$\frac{17}{64}$	6.746875	$\frac{49}{64}$	19.446880
$\frac{9}{32}$	7.143750	$\frac{25}{32}$	19.843750
$\frac{19}{64}$	7.540625	$\frac{51}{64}$	20.240630
$\frac{5}{16}$	7.937500	$\frac{13}{16}$	20.637500
$\frac{21}{64}$	8.334375	$\frac{53}{64}$	21.034380
$\frac{11}{32}$	8.731250	$\frac{27}{32}$	21.431250
$\frac{23}{64}$	9.128125	$\frac{55}{64}$	21.828130
$\frac{3}{8}$	9.525000	$\frac{7}{8}$	22.225000
$\frac{25}{64}$	9.921875	$\frac{57}{64}$	22.621880
$\frac{13}{32}$	10.318750	$\frac{29}{32}$	23.018750
$\frac{27}{64}$	10.715630	$\frac{59}{64}$	23.415630
$\frac{7}{16}$	11.112500	$\frac{15}{16}$	23.812500
$\frac{29}{64}$	11.509380	$\frac{61}{64}$	24.209380
$\frac{15}{32}$	11.906250	$\frac{31}{32}$	24.606250
$\frac{31}{64}$	12.303130	$\frac{63}{64}$	25.003130
$\frac{1}{2}$	12.700000	$\frac{1}{1}$	25.400000

Metric to U.S. Decimal Equivalents

Metric (millimeters)	U.S. Decimal Equivalents (inches)	Metric (millimeters)	U.S. Decimal Equivalents (inches)
1	.03937	14	.55118
2	.07874	15	.59055
3	.11811	16	.62992
4	.15748	17	.66929
5	.19685	18	.70866
6	.23622	19	.74803
7	.27559	20	.78740
8	.31496	21	.82677
9	.35433	22	.86614
10	.39370	23	.90551
11	.43307	24	.94488
12	.47244	25	.98425
13	.51181	26	1.02362

U.S. WEIGHTS AND MEASURES

LENGTH
1 mil = .001 inch
1000 mils = 1 inch = 0.08333 foot
12 inches = 1 foot = 0.33333 yard
3 feet = 1 yard = 36 inches
$5\frac{1}{2}$ yards = 1 rod = $16\frac{1}{2}$ feet

SQUARE MEASURE (AREA)
1 square inch = 0.00694 square foot = 0.00077 square yard
144 square inches = 1 square foot = 0.11111 square yard
9 square feet = 1 square yard = 1296 square inches
$30\frac{1}{4}$ square yards = 1 square rod = .00625 acre

CUBIC MEASURE (VOLUME)
1 cubic inch = .00058 cubic foot = .00002 cubic yard
1728 cubic inches = 1 cubic foot = .03704 cubic yard
27 cubic feet = 1 cubic yard = 46.656 cubic inches
128 cubic feet = 1 cord = 4.736 cubic yards

CAPACITY: LIQUID MEASURE
60 minims = 1 fluidram = .22559 cubic inch
8 fluidrams = 1 fluid ounce = 1.80469 cubic inches
4 fluid ounces = 1 gill = 7.21875 cubic inches
4 gills = 1 pint = 28.875 cubic inches
2 pints = 1 quart = 57.75 cubic inches
4 quarts = 1 gallon = 231 cubic inches
$31\frac{1}{2}$ gallons = 1 barrel = 7277 cubic inches

CAPACITY: DRY MEASURE
1 pint = $\frac{1}{2}$ quart = 33.6 cubic inches
2 pints = 1 quart = 67.2 cubic inches
8 quarts = 1 peck = 537.6 cubic inches
4 pecks = 1 bushel = 2150.4 cubic inches

WEIGHT (AVOIRDUPOIS)
27.344 grains = 1 dram = 0.0625 ounce
16 drams = 1 ounce = 437.5 grains
16 ounces = 1 pound = 7000 grains
25 pounds = 1 quarter = 400 ounces
100 pounds = 1 short hundredweight = 0.05 short ton
112 pounds = 1 long hundredweight = 0.05 long ton
20 short hundredweight = 1 short ton = 2000 pounds
20 long hundredweight = 1 long ton = 2240 pounds

METRIC WEIGHTS AND MEASURES

LENGTH
1 millimeter = 0.001 meter
10 millimeters = 1 centimeter = 0.01 meters
10 centimeters = 1 decimeter = 0.10 meters
10 decimeters = 1 meter
10 meters = 1 dekameter
10 dekameters = 1 hectometer = 100 meters
10 hectometers = 1 kilometer = 1000 meters

SQUARE MEASURE (AREA)
100 square millimeters = 1 square centimeter = 0.0001 square meters
100 square centimeters = 1 square decimeter = 0.01 square meters
100 square decimeters = 1 square meter
100 square meters = 1 are
100 square dekameters = hectare = 10,000 square meters

CUBIC MEASURE (VOLUME)
1000 cubic millimeters = 1 cubic centimeter = 0.000001 cubic meters
1000 cubic centimeters = 1 cubic decimeters = 0.001 cubic meters
1000 cubic decimeters = 1 cubic meter

CAPACITY
10 milliliters = 1 centiliter = 0.01 liter
10 centiliters = 1 deciliter = 0.10 liter
10 deciliters = 1 liter
10 liters = 1 dekaliter
10 dekaliters = 1 hectoliter = 100 liters
10 hectoliters = 1 kiloliter = 1000 liters

WEIGHT
10 milligrams = 1 centigram = 0.01 gram
10 centigrams = 1 decigram = 0.10 gram
10 decigrams = 1 gram
10 grams = 1 dekagram
10 dekagrams = 1 hectogram = 100 grams
10 hectograms = 1 kilogram = 1000 grams
100 kilograms = 1 quintal = 100,000 grams
10 quintals = 1 metric ton = 1,000,000 grams

U.S. AND METRIC EQUIVALENTS

LENGTH
1 inch = 25.4 millimeters = 2.54 centimeters = .0254 meters
1 foot = 304.80 millimeters = 30.48 centimeters = .3048 meter
1 yard = 914.40 millimeters = 91.44 centimeters = .9144 meter
1 millimeter = .03937 inches = .00328084 feet = .00109361 yards
1 centimeter = .39370 inches = .03280840 feet = .01093613 yards
1 meter = 39.37 inches = 3.28084 feet = 1.093613 yards

SQUARE MEASURE (AREA)
1 square inch = 645.16 square millimeters = 6.4516 square centimeters = .00064516 square meter
1 square foot = 92,903 square millimeters = 929.03 square centimeters = .092903 square meter
1 square yard = 836,127 square millimeters = 8,361.27 square centimeters = .836127 square meter
1 square millimeter = .0015500 square inches
1 square centimeter = .155000 square inches = .001076 square feet
1 square meter = 1550.00 square inches = 10.7639 square feet = 1.19599 square yards

CUBIC MEASURE (VOLUME)
1 cubic inch = 16,387 cubic millimeters = 16.3871 cubic centimeters
1 cubic foot = 28,317 cubic centimeters = .0283168 cubic meter
1 cubic yard = .7645549 cubic meter
1 cubic millimeter = .000061 cubic inches
1 cubic centimeter = .06102 cubic inches
1 cubic meter = 35.314 cubic feet = 1.3079 cubic yards

CAPACITY
1 minim = .061610 milliliter = 0.0000616 liter
1 fluidram = 3.6967 milliliters = 0.0036967 liter
1 fluid ounce = 29.5729 milliliters = 0.0295729 liter
1 gill = 118.294 milliliters = 0.118294 liter
1 pint (liquid) = 473.176 milliliters = 0.473176 liter
1 quart (liquid) = 946.35 milliliters = 0.94635 liter
1 gallon (liquid) = 3785.4 milliliters = 3.7854 liters
1 milliliter = 0.27 fluidram = 0.06102 cubic inch
1 centiliter = 0.338 fluid ounce = 0.61020 cubic inch
1 deciliter = 0.21 pint (liquid) = 6.10200 cubic inches
1 liter = 1.057 quarts (liquid) = 61.0200 cubic inches
1 dekaliter = 2.64 gallons (liquid) = 609.840 cubic inches

WEIGHT

1 grain = 0.0648 gram
1 dram (avoirdupois) = 1.77185 grams
1 ounce (avoirdupois) = 28.3495 grams
1 pound (avoirdupois) = 0.4536 kilogram
1 short hundredweight = 45.359 kilograms
1 long hundredweight = 50.802 kilograms
1 short ton = .90718 metric ton
1 long ton = 1.0161 metric tons

ROMAN NUMERALS

Roman Numeral	Arabic Numerals	Roman Numeral	Arabic Numerals
I	1	XXIV	24
II	2	XXV	25
III	3	XXVI	26
IV	4	XXVII	27
V	5	XXVIII	28
VI	6	XXIX	29
VII	7	XXX	30
VIII	8	XL	40
IX	9	L	50
X	10	LX	60
XI	11	LXX	70
XII	12	LXXX	80
XIII	13	XC	90
XIV	14	C	100
XV	15	CC	200
XVI	16	CCC	300
XVII	17	CD	400
XVIII	18	D	500
XIX	19	DC	600
XX	20	DCC	700
XXI	21	DCCC	800
XXII	22	CM	900
XXIII	23	M	1000

CONVERSION TABLE

Note: British imperial measure (liquid and dry) is not shown. (1 British imperial gallon = 1.2009 U.S. gallons)

TO COVERT FROM:	TO:	MULTIPLY BY:
centigrams	grains	0.15432
	grams	0.01
centiliters	fluidrams	2.705
	fluid ounces	0.338147
	liters	0.01
centimeters	feet	0.03281
	inches	0.3937
	meters	0.01
	milliliters	1.00
	mils	393.7
cubic centimeters	cubic feet	0.000035312
	cubic inches	0.06102
	liters	0.001
	cubic meters	0.000001
cubic decimeters	cubic centimeters	1000.0
	cubic inches	61.0237
cubic feet	cubic centimeters	28,317.00
	cubic inches	1728.0
	cubic yards	0.03704
	cubic meters	0.02832
	gallons (liquid)	7.48052
	liters	28.31687
cubic inches	cubic centimeters	16.3872
	cubic feet	0.000579
	cubic meters	0.00001639
	gallons (liquid)	0.00433
	liters	0.01639
	pints (dry)	0.02976
	pints (liquid)	0.03463
	quarts (dry)	0.01488
	quarts (liquid)	0.01732

CONVERSION TABLE (CONTINUED)

TO COVERT FROM:	TO:	MULTIPLY BY:
cubic meters	cubic centimeters	1,000,000.0
	cubic feet	35.314
	cubic inches	61,023.4
	gallons (liquid)	264.17
cubic millimeters	cubic centimeters	0.001
	cubic inches	0.00006
cubic yards	cubic feet	27.0
	cubic inches	46,656.0
	cubic meters	0.7646
decigrams	grains	1.5432
	grams	0.1
deciliters	fluid ounces	3.38
	liters	0.1
decimeters	inches	3.937
	meters	0.1
dekagrams	grams	10.0
	ounces (avoirdupois)	0.3527
dekaliters	gallons (liquid)	2.64
	liters	10.0
dekameters	inches	393.7
	meters	10.0
drams (avoirdupois)	ounces (avoirdupois)	0.0625
	grains	27.3437
	grams	1.7718
drams (liquid)	see fluidrams	
feet	centimeters	30.4801
	inches	12.0
	meters	.3048
	yards	0.3333

CONVERSION TABLE (CONTINUED)

TO COVERT FROM:	TO:	MULTIPLY BY:
fluidrams	cubic inches	0.22559
	fluid ounces	0.125
	milliliters	3.69669
	minims	60.0
fluid ounces	cubic inches	1.80469
	fluidrams	8.0
	gallons (liquid)	0.00781
	liters	0.02959
gallons (dry)	cubic feet	0.1556
	cubic inches	268.8
	cubic meters	0.0044
gallons (liquid)	cubic feet	0.1337
	cubic inches	231.0
	cubic meters	0.0038
	fluid ounces	128.0
	liters	3.7854
gills	pints (liquid)	0.25
grains	drams (avoirdupois)	0.03657
	grams	0.0648
	milligrams	64.7989
	ounces (avoirdupois)	0.00229
	pounds (avoirdupois)	0.00014
grams	grains	15.432
	kilograms	0.001
	milligrams	1000.0
	ounces (avoirdupois)	0.03527
	pounds (avoirdupois)	0.0022
hectograms	grams	100.0
	ounces (avoirdupois)	3.5274
hectoliters	gallons (liquid)	26.418
	liters	100.0

CONVERSION TABLE (CONTINUED)

TO COVERT FROM:	TO:	MULTIPLY BY:
inches	centimeters	2.54
	feet	0.08333
	meters	0.0254
	mils	1000.0
	yards	0.02778
kilograms	grains	15,432.36
	grams	1000.0
	ounces (avoirdupois)	35.274
	pounds (avoirdupois)	2.2046
kiloliters	gallons (liquid)	264.172
	liters	1000.0
kilometers	feet	3,280.833
	meters	1000.0
	miles (statute)	0.62137
liters	cubic centimeters	1000.0
	cubic feet	0.035313
	cubic inches	61.02398
	quarts (dry)	0.9081
	quarts (liquid)	1.0567
	gallons (dry)	0.22702
	gallons (liquid)	0.26417
long tons	pounds (avoirdupois)	2240.0
meters	feet	3.2808
	inches	39.37
	kilometers	.001
	millimeters	1000.0
microns (micrometers)	inches	0.0000394
	meters	0.000001
	mils	0.03937
miles (statute)	feet	5280.0
	kilometers	1.609344

CONVERSION TABLE (CONTINUED)

TO COVERT FROM:	TO:	MULTIPLY BY:
milligrams	grains	0.01543
	grams	0.001
milliliters	fluid ounces	0.0338
	fluidrams	0.2705
	liters	0.001
	cubic centimeters	1.00
millimeters	inches	0.03937
	meters	0.001
	microns	1000.0
	mils	39.37
mils	inches	0.001
	microns	25.4001
	millimeters	0.0254
minims	fluidrams	0.01667
	milliliters	0.06161
ounces (avoirdupois)	drams (avoirdupois)	16.0
	grains	437.5
	grams	28.350
	pounds (avoirdupois)	0.0625
ounces (liquid)	see fluid ounces	
pints (dry)	cubic inches	33.6003
	liters	0.5506
	quarts (dry)	0.5
pints (liquid)	cubic inches	28.875
	gills	4.0
	liters	0.47318
pounds (avoirdupois)	grams	453.592
	grains	7000.0
	ounces (avoirdupois)	16.0
quarts (dry)	cubic inches	67.2006
	liters	1.10112
	pints (dry)	2.0

CONVERSION TABLE (CONTINUED)

TO COVERT FROM:	TO:	MULTIPLY BY:
quarts (liquid)	cubic inches	57.75
	liters	0.94636
	pints (liquid)	2.0
square centimeters	square feet	0.001076
	square inches	0.1550
	square millimeters	100.0
square decimeters	square inches	15.5
	square meters	0.01
square dekameters	square meters	100.0
	square yards	119.599
square feet	square centimeters	929.0341
	square inches	144.0
	square meters	0.0929
	square yards	0.1111
square hectometers	square meters	10,000.0
square inches	square centimeters	6.4516
	square feet	0.00694
	square millimeters	645.1625
	square yards	0.00077
square meters	square centimeters	10,000.0
	square feet	10.7639
	square yards	1.1960
square millimeters	square inches	0.00155
	square meters	0.000001
square yards	square feet	9.0
	square inches	1296.0
	square meters	0.83613
yards	feet	3.0
	inches	36.0
	meters	0.9144

Table of Powers and Roots

Fraction (in lowest terms) Or Whole Number	Decimal Equivalent	Square	Cube	Square Root	Cube Root
$\frac{1}{64}$	.015625	.0002441	.000003815	.125	.25
$\frac{1}{32}$	.03125	.0009766	.000030518	.176777	.31498
$\frac{3}{64}$	.046875	.0021973	.000102997	.216506	.36056
$\frac{1}{16}$	.0625	.0039063	.00024414	.25	.39685
$\frac{5}{64}$	.078125	.0061035	.00047684	.279508	.42749
$\frac{3}{32}$	.09375	.0087891	.00082398	.306186	.45428
$\frac{7}{64}$	.109375	.0119629	.0013084	.330719	.47823
$\frac{1}{8}$	.125	.0156250	.0019531	.353553	.5
$\frac{9}{64}$	.140625	.0197754	.0027809	.375	.52002
$\frac{5}{32}$	.15625	.0244141	.0038147	.395285	.53861
$\frac{11}{64}$	.171875	.0295410	.0050774	.414578	.55600
$\frac{3}{16}$	.1875	.0351563	.0065918	.433013	.57236
$\frac{13}{64}$	.203125	.0412598	.0083809	.450694	.58783
$\frac{7}{32}$	.21875	.0478516	.010468	.467707	.60254
$\frac{15}{64}$	.234375	.0549316	.012875	.484123	.61655
$\frac{1}{4}$	.25	.0625	.015625	.5	.62996
$\frac{17}{64}$	.265625	.0705566	.018742	.515388	.64282
$\frac{9}{32}$	.28125	.0791016	.022247	.530330	.65519
$\frac{19}{64}$	.296875	.0881348	.026165	.544862	.66710
$\frac{5}{16}$	.3125	.0976562	.030518	.559017	.67860
$\frac{21}{64}$	.328125	.107666	.035328	.572822	.68973
$\frac{11}{32}$	.34375	.118164	.040619	.586302	.70051
$\frac{23}{64}$	.359375	.129150	.046413	.599479	.71097
$\frac{3}{8}$	.375	.140625	.052734	.612372	.72113
$\frac{25}{64}$	.390625	.1525879	.059605	.625	.73100
$\frac{13}{32}$	.40625	.1650391	.067047	.637377	.74062
$\frac{27}{64}$	.421875	.1779785	.075085	.649519	.75
$\frac{7}{16}$	.4375	.1914063	.083740	.661438	.75915
$\frac{29}{64}$	.453125	.2053223	.093037	.673146	.76808
$\frac{15}{32}$	.46875	.2197266	.102997	.684653	.77681
$\frac{31}{64}$	.484375	.2346191	.113644	.695971	.78535
$\frac{1}{2}$	.5	.25	.125	.707107	.79370
$\frac{33}{64}$	.515625	.265869	.137089	.718070	.80188
$\frac{17}{32}$	.53125	.282227	.149933	.728869	.80990
$\frac{35}{64}$	.546875	.299072	.163555	.739510	.81777
$\frac{9}{16}$	.5625	.316406	.177979	.75	.82548
$\frac{37}{64}$	.578125	.334229	.193226	.760345	.83306
$\frac{19}{32}$	.59375	.352539	.209320	.770552	.84049
$\frac{39}{64}$	.609375	.371338	.226284	.780625	.84780
$\frac{5}{8}$	.625	.390625	.244141	.790569	.85499
$\frac{41}{64}$	.640625	.410400	.262913	.800391	.86205
$\frac{21}{32}$	.65625	.430664	.282623	.810093	.86901
$\frac{43}{64}$	.671875	.451416	.303295	.819680	.87585
$\frac{11}{16}$	.6875	.472656	.324951	.829156	.88259

Table of Powers and Roots

Fraction (in lowest terms) Or Whole Number	Decimal Equivalent	Square	Cube	Square Root	Cube Root
$\frac{45}{64}$	.703125	.494385	.347614	.838525	.88922
$\frac{23}{32}$	.71875	.516602	.371307	.847791	.89576
$\frac{47}{64}$	.734375	.539307	.396053	.856957	.90221
$\frac{3}{4}$	.75	.5625	.421875	.866025	.90856
$\frac{49}{64}$	.765625	.586182	.448795	.875	.91483
$\frac{25}{32}$	.78125	.610352	.476837	.883883	.92101
$\frac{51}{64}$	.796875	.635010	.506023	.892679	.92711
$\frac{13}{16}$	.8125	.660156	.536377	.901388	.93313
$\frac{53}{64}$	.828125	.685791	.567921	.910014	.93907
$\frac{27}{32}$	.84375	.711914	.600677	.918559	.94494
$\frac{55}{64}$	.859375	.738525	.634670	.927025	.95074
$\frac{7}{8}$	.875	.765625	.669922	.935414	.95647
$\frac{57}{64}$	.890625	.793213	.706455	.943729	.96213
$\frac{29}{32}$	.90625	.821289	.744293	.951972	.96772
$\frac{59}{64}$	.921875	.849854	.783459	.960143	.97325
$\frac{15}{16}$	.9375	.878906	.823975	.968246	.97872
$\frac{61}{64}$	.953125	.908447	.865864	.976281	.98412
$\frac{31}{32}$	.96875	.938477	.909149	.984251	.98947
$\frac{63}{64}$	.984375	.968994	.953854	.992157	.99476
1	1.000000	1	1	1.00000	1.00000
2	2.000000	4	8	1.41421	1.25992
3	3.000000	9	27	1.73205	1.44225
4	4.000000	16	64	2.00000	1.58740
5	5.000000	25	125	2.23607	1.70998
6	6.000000	36	216	2.44949	1.81712
7	7.000000	49	343	2.64575	1.91293
8	8.000000	64	512	2.82843	2.00000
9	9.000000	81	729	3.00000	2.08008
10	10.000000	100	1000	3.16228	2.15443
11	11.000000	121	1331	3.31662	2.22398
12	12.000000	144	1728	3.46410	2.28943
13	13.000000	169	2197	3.60555	2.35133
14	14.000000	196	2744	3.74166	2.41014
15	15.000000	225	3375	3.87298	2.46621
16	16.000000	256	4096	4.00000	2.51984
17	17.000000	289	4913	4.12311	2.57128
18	18.000000	324	5832	4.24264	2.62074
19	19.000000	361	6859	4.35890	2.66840
20	20.000000	400	8000	4.47214	2.71442
21	21.000000	441	9261	4.58258	2.75892
22	22.000000	484	10,648	4.69042	2.80204
23	23.000000	529	12,167	4.79583	2.84387
24	24.000000	576	13,824	4.89898	2.88450
25	25.000000	625	15,625	5.00000	2.92402

Table of Powers and Roots

Fraction (in lowest terms) Or Whole Number	Decimal Equivalent	Square	Cube	Square Root	Cube Root
26	26.000000	676	17,576	5.09902	2.96250
27	27.000000	729	19,683	5.19615	3.00000
28	28.000000	784	21,952	5.29150	3.03659
29	29.000000	841	24,389	5.38516	3.07232
30	30.000000	900	27,000	5.47723	3.10723
31	31.000000	961	29,791	5.56776	3.14138
32	32.000000	1024	32,768	5.65685	3.17480
33	33.000000	1089	35,937	5.74456	3.20753
34	34.000000	1156	39,304	5.83095	3.23961
35	35.000000	1225	42,875	5.91608	3.27107
36	36.000000	1296	46,656	6.00000	3.30193
37	37.000000	1369	50,653	6.08276	3.33222
38	38.000000	1444	54,872	6.16441	3.36198
39	39.000000	1521	59,319	6.24500	3.39121
40	40.000000	1600	64,000	6.32456	3.41995
41	41.000000	1681	68,921	6.40312	3.44822
42	42.000000	1764	74,088	6.48074	3.47603
43	43.000000	1849	79,507	6.55744	3.50340
44	44.000000	1936	85,184	6.63325	3.53035
45	45.000000	2025	91,125	6.70820	3.55689
46	46.000000	2116	97,336	6.78233	3.58305
47	47.000000	2209	103,823	6.85565	3.60883
48	48.000000	2304	110,592	6.92820	3.63424
49	49.000000	2401	117,649	7.00000	3.65931
50	50.000000	2500	125,000	7.07107	3.68403
51	51.000000	2601	132,651	7.14143	3.70843
52	52.000000	2704	140,608	7.21110	3.73251
53	53.000000	2809	148,877	7.28011	3.75629
54	54.000000	2916	157,464	7.34847	3.77976
55	55.000000	3025	166,375	7.41620	3.80295
56	56.000000	3136	175,616	7.48331	3.82586
57	57.000000	3249	185,193	7.54983	3.84850
58	58.000000	3364	195,112	7.61577	3.87088
59	59.000000	3481	205,379	7.68115	3.89300
60	60.000000	3600	216,000	7.74597	3.91487
61	61.000000	3721	226,981	7.81025	3.93650
62	62.000000	3844	238,328	7.87401	3.95789
63	63.000000	3969	250,047	7.93725	3.97906
64	64.000000	4096	262,144	8.00000	4.00000
65	65.000000	4225	274,625	8.06226	4.02073
66	66.000000	4356	287,496	8.12404	4.04124
67	67.000000	4489	300,763	8.18535	4.06155
68	68.000000	4624	314,432	8.24621	4.08166
69	69.000000	4761	328,509	8.30662	4.10157

Table of Powers and Roots

Fraction (in lowest terms) Or Whole Number	Decimal Equivalent	Square	Cube	Square Root	Cube Root
70	70.000000	4900	343,000	8.36660	4.12129
71	71.000000	5041	357,911	8.42615	4.14082
72	72.000000	5184	373,248	8.48528	4.16017
73	73.000000	5329	389,017	8.54400	4.17934
74	74.000000	5476	405,224	8.60233	4.19834
75	75.000000	5625	421,875	8.66025	4.21716
76	76.000000	5776	438,976	8.71780	4.23582
77	77.000000	5929	456,533	8.77496	4.25432
78	78.000000	6084	474,552	8.83176	4.27266
79	79.000000	6241	493,039	8.88819	4.29084
80	80.000000	6400	512,000	8.94427	4.30887
81	81.000000	6561	531,441	9.00000	4.32675
82	82.000000	6724	551,368	9.05539	4.34448
83	83.000000	6889	571,787	9.11043	4.36207
84	84.000000	7056	592,704	9.16515	4.37952
85	85.000000	7225	614,125	9.21954	4.39683
86	86.000000	7396	636,056	9.27362	4.41400
87	87.000000	7569	658,503	9.32738	4.43105
88	88.000000	7744	681,472	9.38083	4.44796
89	89.000000	7921	704,969	9.43398	4.46475
90	90.000000	8100	729,000	9.48683	4.48140
91	91.000000	8281	753,571	9.53939	4.49794
92	92.000000	8464	778,688	9.59166	4.51436
93	93.000000	8649	804,357	9.64365	4.53065
94	94.000000	8836	830,584	9.69536	4.54684
95	95.000000	9025	857,375	9.74679	4.56290
96	96.000000	9216	884,736	9.79796	4.57886
97	97.000000	9409	912,673	9.84886	4.59470
98	98.000000	9604	941,192	9.89949	4.61044
99	99.000000	9801	970,299	9.94987	4.62607
100	100.000000	10,000	1,000,000	10.00000	4.64159

Index